The Simple Life

The Simple Life

THE CHRISTIAN STANCE
TOWARD POSSESSIONS

as taught by Jesus
interpreted by Kierkegaard
and presented now by

VERNARD ELLER

WILLIAM B. EERDMANS PUBLISHING COMPANY
GRAND RAPIDS, MICHIGAN

Library of Congress Cataloging in Publication Data

Eller, Vernard.
  The simple life; the Christian stance toward possessions.

Includes bibliographical references.
1. Simplicity.   2. Jesus Christ—Teachings.
3. Kierkegaard, Søren Aabye, 1813-1855.   I. Title.
BJ1496.E36   248'.4   73-6589
ISBN 0-8028-1537-5

The selections from CHRISTIAN DISCOURSES by Søren Kierkegaard, translated by Walter Lowrie, are here reprinted by the kind permission of the Rev. Mr. Howard A. Johnson.

The selections from FOR SELF-EXAMINATION AND JUDGE FOR YOURSELVES by Søren Kierkegaard, translated, with an introduction, by Walter Lowrie (Princeton University Press, 1944), are reprinted by permission of Princeton University Press.

Scripture quotations are, unless otherwise indicated, from THE NEW ENGLISH BIBLE. Copyright © The Delegates of the Oxford University Press and the Syndics of the Cambridge University Press 1961, 1970. Reprinted by permission.

In memory of one
whose labyrinthine life,
by the grace of God,
did come to be
simply put:

SØREN KIERKEGAARD

CONTENTS

Chapter One

IF IT'S THE SIMPLE LIFE, WHY DOES IT HAVE TO BE SO COMPLICATED?

Simply put, it's the life! And that being so, one would think that the book about it could be simple as well.

By "the simple life," we are going to start saying now and continue saying until the very end, we mean to designate that stance toward possessions and "things" that was recommended, taught, and practiced by Jesus — only this and nothing other than this, even though something other might seem to qualify under the rubric. This is to say that our entire discussion will assume the Christian orientation of both author and reader and take place within that context. No opinion will be expressed regarding what values or possibilities there might be in a non-Christian "simple life." A book on that subject *could* be written (and many have been) ; but this is not one of them. Our interest is the *Christian* understanding of the simple life.

One may say: "And such a qualification should have the effect of making the discussion just that much more simple."

It does. And the Christian doctrine of the simple life would be simplicity itself, except

1: if we let it get too simple we won't have the where-withal for a book.

2: the Christian teaching is by nature *dialectical*.

3: the people who are supposed to be following the teaching are human beings.

This matter of "dialectics" is going to be with us all the way, so let us get it well in hand right here at the beginning. Thinking becomes "dialectical" when it finds itself being pulled two ways at once, finds it necessary to give weight and attention to two different and apparently opposed poles of thought.

The best picture of "dialectic" I can propose is a demonstration seen frequently in appliance and department stores. The store wants to call attention to its vacuum cleaners and so rigs one with the hose pointed upward and the machine turned on "blow." In the jet of air above the nozzle rides a pingpong ball, dancing imponderably in space. Actually, the ball is caught in the balance between two opposing forces. Gravity is at work to pull it *down*. But when the ball gives way to that gravity and does come down, this brings it that much closer to the source of the air jet, which has the effect of blowing it *up*. Yet, when the ball assents to that force and goes up, it quickly gets out of range to the point where gravity takes over again and pulls it back down.

(For those who appreciate a bit of sophistication in their theology, it can be said that it is the Bernoulli Principle that keeps the ball from slipping out sideways. In theology, then, it is the Sin Principle that *enables* people to slip out sideways — which is why so many more people than pingpong balls are lost and physics is so much more of an exact science than theology is.)

Plainly, the ball is not *fixed* in place but can stay in place only as long as it continues dancing in and out of place. Thought (or action) that operates out of this sort of dynamic tension, giving attention to one truth in such a way that attention must then immediately be given to its counterpart — this is what we mean by "dialectic."

Of course, the simple life is by no means the only dialectical teaching to be found in Christianity; and, indeed, we will discover several different dialectics operating within the simple life itself. However, the most central one is this: essentially, the simple life is the believer's *inner* relationship to God finding expression in his *outward* relationship to "things."

This is what might be called a "weighted dialectic," in that it clearly is the first pole that takes priority, is determinative and all-controlling, and is in fact the source that gives rise to the second pole. Yet, even though the pole of outward expression is secondary, it is absolutely essential; this is a true dialectic. If someone were to claim that the simple life is that life which wants to go all the way with inner relationship to God and so deny the need for appropriate outward expression, that would be proof enough that the inner relationship itself lacks probity. But on the other hand, there is no sort of outward expression that, in and of itself, can be taken as proof that the inner relationship is true. There is no alternative but to keep both elements in view simultaneously. At every step our consideration of the simple life must dance back and forth between the inner relationship to God and the outward relationship to "things," each move toward one pole calling for a corrective move toward the other.

The plan for this book called for Søren Kierkegaard to be brought into play only in the second part; but because he has a parable that gets to the very heart of what Christianity understands by the simple life — and because it so

beautifully underlines the point we are making — we
have chosen to give him a piece of the action here.

> When the prosperous man on a dark but star-lit night
> drives comfortably in his carriage and has the lanterns
> lighted, aye, then he is safe, he fears no difficulty, he
> carries his light with him, and it is not dark close around
> him; but precisely because he has the lanterns lighted,
> and has a strong light close to him, precisely for this
> reason he cannot see the stars, for his lights obscure the
> stars, which the poor peasant driving without lights can
> see gloriously in the dark but starry night. So those
> deceived ones live in the temporal existence: either,
> occupied with the necessities of life, they are too busy to
> avail themselves of the view, or in their prosperity and
> good days they have, as it were, lanterns lighted, and
> close about them everything is so satisfactory, so pleasant,
> so comfortable — but the view is lacking, the prospect,
> the view of the stars.[1]

Clearly, "the view of the stars" here intends one's awareness and enjoyment of God — which is, of course, an *inner*
relationship. Yet notice that the intensity of lantern light
cannot be equated simply with a person's financial worth.
Kierkegaard elsewhere specifies that one's *concern* over
what may be the *little* he owns or, for that matter, his
concern over precisely that which he does *not* own but
would like to — these concerns can be just as obstructive
of the star view as can the actual owning itself.

Likewise, the parable does not necessarily demand the
extinguishing of each and every carriage lantern; from one
source or another the horses need at least enough light to
see where they are going; and in our day and age, if not in
Kierkegaard's, the law would require enough of a running

---

[1]Kierkegaard, *The Gospel of Suffering*, trans. by David and Lillian
Swenson (Augsburg Publishing House), p. 123.

light to keep the carriage from being run down. And even more so with the simple life than with the carriage, it will be completely impossible to set down a hard, fast, universally applicable law as to how much lantern light is contributive and how much constitutes an obscuring of the view.

And then consider that the extinguishing of lanterns in itself in no way insures that the rider will in fact catch the view of the stars; there always is the possibility that he may keep his face only to the ground. There just is *no* outward arrangement that can stand as a guarantee of the inner relationship. Actually, the matter probably will want to go both ways: the rider catches a glimpse of the stars, which moves him to blow out his lanterns, and the dousing of the lanterns serves to enhance his view of the stars. This is what it means to be dialectical.

But that the doctrine of the simple life is by nature dialectical means only that the concept is *complex* rather than *simple* (in the technical meaning of those terms) ; it is not to say that either the understanding or the practice of it must be *complicated*. That is true; the complicating aspect comes in the fact that the understanding and the practice have to be accomplished by human beings. And because of their profound comprehension of and stalwart adherence to the Sin Principle, the first thing that has to be said about human beings is that, if they possibly can find a way of working things to their own advantage, they will do it.

So someone will say: "O.K. You say that the essence of the simple life is an inner relationship. I'll buy that. I've got the relationship; I love God like nobody's business. And it is nobody's business but mine! You can't say that I don't love God. You've already admitted that there are no outward signs that can prove whether or not one has a view of the stars — and I'm telling you that I see them. So get off my back about my standard of living; I don't own anything but what I need, and I'm just as good a Christian as anyone else. And by the way, what kind of car is it that *you* drive?"

The dialectic of the simple life leaves itself wide open for misuse by those who want credit for living it but who are in no way inclined to change their style of life.

But the misuse can go the other way just as easily: "All right! The simple life involves a particular manner and level of living. Very good. You just define that way of life for me; put it down in a 1-2-3 order, and I will set about conforming to those standards. Of course, once I have done it I will expect you to recognize the achievement and credit me as the righteous Christian I am. After all, what would be the sense of making all these sacrifices unless I get something in return?"

The dialectic of the simple life also leaves itself wide open for misuse by the sort of legalism and works-righteousness that would earn credit for living it without even realizing what it means to have a view of the stars.

So complaint is always possible: "It's got to be one way or the other. You say which, and we'll be happy to go along. But you've got to make up your mind. If the simple life is an inner attitude, we'll play it that way. If it is a visible and concrete mode of life, we'll operate accordingly. But come on, you've got to say which!"

It is the universal human ingenuity at taking advantage of a situation — including the double-endedness of a dialectic — that makes the simple life so complicated. In the same way it makes complicated the writing of this book. When I rush over to shut off the escape hatch at one end of the dialectic, that inevitably leaves unguarded the hatch at the other end; but to run back to that end necessarily is to desert this end. If we come down too strongly on the simple life as inner relationship, we say something false. But if we emphasize it as being an outward mode of living, we also say something false. This subject isn't going to be easy, so I beg the reader to be as helpful as he can.

Our purpose is not simply to help us *think* dialectically or to comprehend a dialectical thesis; it is to help us (you, the reader, and me, the writer) feel, act, and be like a dancing pingpong ball regarding our own manner of life. This means that we need to become suspicious of ourselves — particularly when we feel complacent about the style in which we are living or to which we aspire. Most of all, we need to suspect ourselves whenever there arises an urge to escape the tension and flee to either one pole or the other as a means of justifying ourselves and our chosen way of life. I will confess that the writing of this book makes me uncomfortable; I hope that you are willing to share the dialectical discomfort with me.

Finally, a word should be said to the effect that this leaving of itself wide open for misuse is not a defect nor is it anything unique to the doctrine of the simple life; it is a hallmark of the gospel itself. After all, that gospel centers upon a Saviour who was absurdly easy to crucify; it has to do with the *free* grace of God that, as Bonhoeffer pointed out, so easily can be misused as *cheap* grace. Yet this is the way the gospel was meant to be; this leaving of himself vulnerable to misuse is a mark of God's great love toward us. And the goal of that love is that, through it, we each and all of us someday will come to desert the ways of misuse and learn instead to live out of the view, the prospect, the view of the stars.

PART I

According to Jesus and Company

Chapter Two

THE FIRST AND THE REST

The previous chapter was something of a warm-up; now we are ready to go to work in earnest. Part I will be an examination of the simple life as taught by Jesus *and company*. That is to say, we will start with Jesus' teachings in the Gospels but then in subsequent chapters move to some writings of Paul and then to the work of an anonymous author of the early church.

However, even when dealing with the sayings that the Gospels attribute to Jesus, we are not going to make critical-historical judgments as to what represents "the very words of Jesus" and what represents the contribution of subsequent transmitters of the tradition. In point of fact, our interest lies more in "the mind of Christ" than in "the very words of Jesus." Now we are convinced — although it is impossible to prove — that the very words of Jesus do lie in there somewhere as the root and source of the truth we are after. Nevertheless, we proceed upon the faith that, through the help and guidance of the Holy Spirit, the mind of Christ is revealed even in the dedicated efforts of those who came after Jesus — the "company." We will not even try to be scrupulous in maintaining the distinctions as to who is who among them.

The one most crucial statement regarding the simple

life undoubtedly is that which concludes the long passage
on the subject in the Sermon on the Mount:

> *Set your mind on God's kingdom and his justice before
> everything else, and all the rest will come to you as well.*
> —Matthew 6:33

Here is the absolutely essential premise upon which
thought, faith, and practice must build if the result is to
qualify as the simple life in any *Christian* sense. There is
a "first," and there is an "all the rest." The gospel never
attempts to deny the reality or validity of the "all the rest."
Nevertheless, a hard and fast distinction is to be maintained between them; no confusion can be allowed.

The all-controlling consideration must be that the
"first" actually is made first and maintained as first. Once
that is done, "all the rest" can come along behind, find its
place, and assume true value and authenticity; this is
Christianity's "simple life." However, just as soon as any
item — any item at all — out of "the rest" is taken as a
value in and of itself, independent of, in competition with,
or as a replacement for the true "first," then the result
may look good, be nice, make sense, and give satisfaction,
but the situation nevertheless has been moved entirely out
of the sphere of what Christianity understands as "the
simple life."

As long as *"all* the rest" is so ordered as to "come to you
as well," to come *after,* to come out of and consequent
upon the "first," then it has been provided with the control
that will make it good, keep it good, and use it for good.
But there is nothing — not one thing — in that "all the
rest" that is inherently good enough in itself so that it
can stand in place of or alongside of the "first" without
corrupting its own value and meaning in the process. The
simple life is essentially a matter of putting the "first" first,

and there just is no other place from which one can start
and have any hope of arriving at what Jesus talks about.

And in this instance, the old saying of "putting first
things first" is not quite good enough. The New Testament makes it evident that the "first" of which it speaks
is a singular and not a plural; "putting *the first thing
first*" would be the only proper statement of the matter.
Kierkegaard (whom we have no intention of introducing
yet; he is muscling in — as he does into most of what I
write) has a book entitled *Purity of Heart Is to Will One
Thing*. It could as well have been called (and Kierkegaard
would not object) *The Simple Life Is to Will One Thing*.
But in that book he makes the point that only the "first"
that Jesus here specifies can be put first and remain only
one thing. Anything else that might be taken out of the
"all the rest" and set up as "first" inevitably will result in
doublemindedness rather than a single focus.

Now this "first" is, of course, the inner relationship to
God of which we spoke earlier, "the view of the stars" of
Kierkegaard's parable. We are handling the same dialectic we described then. But now we can begin to speak
much more concretely about what that inner relationship
represents.

"Set your mind on God's kingdom and his justice before
everything else," Jesus tells us. Verbally that might seem
to be a double focus; in actuality it is not. "God's kingdom" does not designate a location or any outward object,
as the bare words *could* be taken to indicate. His *kingdom*
is his "kingness," the *de facto* situation of his being *king,*
his exercising of the rule that is proper to him. Thus, "to
set one's mind upon his kingdom" is to seek, above all,
to let his will be done in one's life, to put oneself into
appropriate relationship to him as a subject to his true and
sovereign Lord.

That we are to seek God's "justice" (righteousness), on
the other hand, does not, in the first place (and we are
concerned here particularly with "the first place," you
will recall), invite us to try to bring the affairs of men into
that arrangement we feel God would deem "just"; this,
properly, is part of the "all the rest that will come to you as
well." No, in the first place, God's "justice" is *his own*
activity of getting things straightened out and made right,
his own "just-making action." Thus, "to set one's mind
upon his justice" is to relate to him in such a way that he
can make *you* right — "let him have his way with thee,"
as the old hymn has it. This, of course, also is to approach
him as true and sovereign Lord; and God's *kingdom* and
his *justice* turn out to be two *words* pointing to one *reality*,
one relationship. The one thing that must be "first" is
fealty, i.e. absolute, personal loyalty.

And this is a matter of *inner* relationship. Why it is so
important to make that specification we shall discover as
we press the line of thought a bit further. Along with these
ideas of "kingdom," "justice," and "fealty," there is, of
course, bound up the idea of "obedience." But we must
be careful to understand what it means to "obey one's
lord." If I do everything he has in mind but do it *because*
I happen to agree that what he has suggested is the in-
telligent and appropriate thing to do, then in actuality I
am not obeying *him*. In reality I am obeying my own good
sense and judgment—which, thus far, happily, has chanced
to coincide with his. But in such case, the *principle* under
which I am operating would say that I am to obey only
as long as his commands strike me as being right and
proper. And this is *not* putting *God's* kingdom and his
justice before everything else; it is putting *myself* first, my
judgments, my ideas of good and bad, of right and wrong.

"Doing the will of God," then, does not mean simply

doing what he wants done; it means doing it "because" *he* wants it done. And that is entirely a matter of *inner* motivation; there is no way (*no* way) by studying the resultant outward actions to determine whether they were performed *because* God wanted them that way or *because*, on my own, I thought it was a good idea. But Jesus is insistent that only the life that springs from the inner motivation of personal loyalty to the Lord God is truly the simple life.

Time after time, Jesus pinpoints the matter here. Each paragraph of this section of the Sermon on the Mount centers on this matter of single loyalty.

> *Do not store up for yourselves treasure on earth, where it grows rusty and moth-eaten, and thieves break in to steal it. Store up treasure in heaven, where there is no moth and no rust to spoil it, no thieves to break in and steal. For where your treasure is, there will your heart be also.* — Matthew 6:19-21

Your "treasure" is that to which you ascribe preeminent value. And what could "treasure in heaven" be except the valuing of God himself and one's personal relationship to him? — treasure, by the way, that is available to be enjoyed even before one is "in heaven." And, we are told, it is upon *this* treasure we are to put our hearts before everything else.

> *The lamp of the body is the eye. If your eyes are sound [single], you will have light for your whole body; if the eyes are bad, your whole body will be in darkness. If then the only light you have is darkness, the darkness is doubly dark.* — Matthew 6:22-23

All of a person's seeing, the illumination of his entire existence, depends entirely upon the focus of his eye (his loyalty commitment), whether it be toward light or darkness. If that focused orientation is not sound and single, not totally upon God, then whatever else in all this world one might wish to see, it will accordingly be darkened. The eye ("I") must be right if anything is rightly to be seen.

> *No servant can be the slave of two masters; for either he will hate the first and love the second, or he will be devoted to the first and think nothing of the second. You cannot serve God and Money.*
> — Matthew 6:24

One's ultimate loyalty must converge at a single point. To try to go two ways at once will rip a person down the middle and make his a multi-manic rather than a simple life.

> *THEREFORE I bid you put away anxious thoughts about food and drink to keep you alive, and clothes to cover your body. . . . All these are things for the heathen to run after, not for you, because your heavenly Father knows that you need them all. Set your mind on God's kingdom and his justice before everything else, and all the rest will come to you as well.*
> — Matthew 6:25, 32-33

Jesus stakes his teaching of the simple life upon one and only one principle, namely, that absolute personal loyalty to God must take precedence over anything and everything else.

We are considering this principle in its particular application regarding a believer's relationship to his possessions, to "things." But Jesus himself applies it much more broadly — to the extent that it becomes apparent that this is indeed one of the major thrusts of his entire teaching ministry. The twelfth chapter of Matthew marks a second concentration on the theme.

> *Every kingdom divided against itself goes to ruin; and*
> *no town, no household, that is divided against itself can*
> *stand.*
>
> — Matthew 12:25
>
> *He who is not with me is against me, and he who does*
> *not gather with me scatters.*
>
> — Matthew 12:30

This latter saying is of special interest, because there is
another saying, in Mark, which would seem to be a direct
contradiction:

> *John said to him, "Master, we saw a man driving out*
> *devils in your name, and as he was not one of us, we*
> *tried to stop him." Jesus said, "Do not stop him; no one*
> *who does a work of divine power in my name will be*
> *able the next moment to speak evil of me. For he who is*
> *not against us is on our side."*
>
> — Mark 9:38-40

Many scholars jump to the conclusion that we have here
two different versions of the same saying. The problem
then becomes to determine which is the original, which
is the way Jesus himself had it. I have no opinion on that
matter; but I think I see how *both* can be true — and how,
if the two are put *together,* they speak a greater truth than
either could singly.

In the first, Jesus is making the same point that we have
been finding elsewhere, namely, that life must center
upon a single loyalty. However, we should give notice to a
difference between this saying and the others. For the
most part Jesus speaks of this loyalty being directed *to*
God, although at times, as here, he speaks rather of loyalty
toward himself. The remainder of the New Testament
tends most often to affect the latter style and speak of
loyal discipleship *to Jesus.*

Actually, there is no conflict at all between these two ways of putting the matter, because, throughout the New Testament, Jesus is presented as being the Christ, the anointed one, the one whom God has *chosen* as the agent of his own presence among men. Thus, when someone wants to be loyal to God, God, as it were, points to Jesus and says, "Very good; and my desire is that you express your loyalty to me by becoming a true disciple of his." And if someone chooses to make Jesus his Lord and dedicate himself loyally to him, Jesus says, "Fine; but to be loyal to me you must be entirely loyal to God as I myself am." There is no way that the two loyalties can get out of balance, because they are, in fact, *one* loyalty.

"He who is not with me is against me": unless one has given his entire personal loyalty to Christ, the overall effect of his activity will be to undercut rather than enhance God's intention for man and the world. But notice that in the second instance (the one from Mark) it twice is specified that the outsider is doing his work "in Jesus' name"; and the emphasis surely is meant to imply that the man's loyalty *is* centered on Jesus. Jesus, then, is saying to his disciples, "If this man's action is motivated by a commitment of loyalty to me, then you have no right to try to dictate what form that commitment must take, through what means it must express itself. For he who is not against us is on our side."

If this interpretation is correct, it says precisely what we have been striving to say regarding the simple life. The "first" of the simple life must be a single-willed centering upon God; there is absolutely no room for variation on this point. But as strongly as the undeviating singularity of that aspect is decreed, just as strongly is it insisted that the means, the "how," the "all the rest," the outward details of its expression, cannot be decreed. No one dare try to tell anyone else what the simple life *has* to look like. For he who is not against us is on our side. Later in the Matthew chapter, Jesus is still on the theme:

> *"Who is my mother? Who are my brothers?"; and pointing to the disciples, he said, "Here are my mother and my brothers. Whoever does the will of my heavenly Father is my brother, my sister, my mother."*
> — Matthew 12:48-50

For Jesus, this loyalty of doing the will of God so entirely takes precedence over everything else that, as he says, the person who practices it comes closer to and rates higher with him than do his own mother, brothers, and sisters.

In the succeeding chapter of Matthew, Jesus stresses the great importance of undivided commitment by presenting twin parables regarding the kingdom of heaven. Recall that this "kingdom of heaven" is God himself affirmed in his kingly ruling.

> *The kingdom of heaven is like treasure lying buried in a field. The man who found it, buried it again; and for sheer joy went and sold everything he had, and bought that field.*
> *Here is another picture of the kingdom of heaven. A merchant looking for fine pearls found one of very special value; so he went and sold everything he had, and bought it.* — Matthew 13:44-46

Finally, in Luke's Gospel, there is a saying of Jesus that puts the matter as pointedly as any statement could:

> *No one who sets his hand to the plough and then keeps looking back is fit for the kingdom of God.*
> — Luke 9:62

It is abundantly clear, first of all, that Jesus demanded as an exclusive priority that a person center his life, loyalty,

and valuations solely upon God. It is clear, in the second
place, that his understanding of the simple life devolves
entirely from this premise. Thus the doctrine of the simple
life is indeed simplicity itself and can be very simply put:
one is living the simple life when his ultimate loyalty is
directed solely to God and when, in consequence, he lets
every other concern flow out of, fall in behind, and witness
to this one. *That* simply it can be put, and *that* simple it
would stay — except for the inveterate human tendency
that works both consciously and unconsciously to take
advantage of the inward invisibility of that prime commitment in order to justify and secure for ourselves modes of
living that do in fact spring from quite contrary motiva-
tions. Thus we *must* give attention to the second half of
Jesus' formula: the "all the rest" that will come to you
as well.

Quite certainly, the "all the rest" Jesus had in mind
consisted of the food, drink, and clothing he mentioned —
plus all sorts of other things a person can own as sources
of pleasure and satisfaction, plus even other things which
a person does not own but which nonetheless are also
resources (such things as air, sunlight, scenery, music,
friends, etc.) .

And we need to take careful note here — although we
will elaborate the point later — that Jesus in no way suggests that these "all the rest" items are inherently evil,
that our lives would be more Christian and our commitment to God truer if we would eliminate as many of them
as possible. Not at all; these things are to "come to you as
well," and it is right and good that they do. The simple
life is not to be equated with the least possible consumption of worldly goods and satisfactions. No, the point is
that these things can be good — very good — *if they are*

*used to support man's relationship to God rather than
compete with it.*

But although Jesus likely had in mind "things," his
basic principle can be applied as well to a different sort of
sample out of the "all the rest," namely, to other motiva-
tions and rationales for simple living. We will look at a
number of these in turn, but our conclusion regarding
each of them will be the same. We will find that each has
some real merit and value *as long as it is kept subordinate
to the ultimate motivation of loyalty to God,* but that none
is able to stand by itself as an adequate or dependable
motive for Christianity's simple life.

Hedonism

This heading may seem strange as the identification of
an argument *for* the simple life; yet it is, perhaps, the
argument most prevalent today. And the term is accurate
for what we have in mind: *hedonism* is the pursuit of or
devotion to pleasure. In this instance the argument goes
that a life style that is marked by the conscious simplifying
of one's possessions, regimen, and relationships is con-
spicuously more satisfying and pleasurable than that which
is devoted to luxury, consumption, and diversion.

Now I firmly believe that this argument has a great deal
of truth in it — at least for many people in many situations.
Even having granted this, however, it must be recognized
that, in our day, in certain sectors of our society this
penchant for simplicity has taken on proportions of a fad
and cult. Simplicity is given a big play in the media, and
peer pressure is brought to bear on people to conform to
this style. But before pop simplicity can be taken as proof
of the hedonistic thesis, it will be necessary to see how
deep is the commitment to this style and how long it lasts;

undeniably, fads do have a way of dying out as quickly as
they spring up.

But grant the current phenomenon as much weight as
you will, there still is no way of guaranteeing to any given
person that *he* would find the simple life enjoyable. I
recently read an article about the super-yachts that compete in the California-Hawaii run. They not only cost a
fortune to acquire but another fortune to maintain and
operate. The reporter asked one owner how he justified
such an expenditure. The answer—very simple and honest
— was that he got a kick out of it, he *enjoyed* owning his
boat and sailing it. And who is to say that the man was
mistaken about his own feelings?

It would seem the height of presumption to insist to a
person, "I'm sorry, but you're not smart enough to know
when you're enjoying yourself. You've got to let me tell
you when you're happy — and that won't be until you are
as I am, until you are living my kind of life style." As I
said, I am confident that there *are* many people who would
be happier if they didn't have so much "stuff" to bother
with; but I am just as confident that there are many other
people who would be perfectly miserable if they had to
give up their prized stuff (whatever it may mean to be
"*perfectly* miserable").

Because of the very subjective nature of "enjoyment,"
then, the hedonistic argument lacks anything in the way
of "teeth" or obligation. If I do happen to find simplicity
satisfying, I should, of course, live it. But if I happen not
to, then there is absolutely no reason — according to the
terms of this argument — why I should have any concern
about the simple life.

Further, the New Testament nowhere so much as hints
that simplicity, in and of itself, brings satisfaction. It is
true that, in connection with the parable of the rich fool,

Luke 12:15 has Jesus saying, "Even when a man has more than enough, his wealth does not give him life." But this is not to say that the renunciation of wealth *will* give him life. Or read it in the Revised Standard Version: "A man's life does not consist in the abundance of his possessions." This is not to say that his life *does* consist in the *limiting* of his possessions. The immediate context of that saying — let alone the total context of the life and teachings of Jesus — makes it plain that a man's life does consist, rather, in his relationship to God.

Similarly, Jesus' key statement definitely did *not* say, "Set your mind on simplicity of life style before everything else, and all the rest will come to you as well." Indeed, if the hedonistic argument is allowed to stand as a self-contained rationale, it is a subversion of Jesus' teaching, for it in fact *is* a being anxious about "what are we to eat? what are we to drink? what shall we wear?" In its emphasis upon finding a stance that is most personally satisfying it is at one with those who have chosen the way of wealth and consumption — differing only in *what* one happens to find most satisfying among the things of the world. Yet a lust for simplicity, in and of itself, is just as little a seeking first of God's kingdom and can be just as obstructive of the view of the stars as the lust for luxury can be.

Now the gospel does have a concern about man's finding satisfaction and enjoyment but comes at this from an angle quite different from insisting that the simple pleasures of life are best. Rather, it is as the Shorter Westminster Catechism puts it so well: "Man's chief end is to glorify God and enjoy him forever." Therefore if because I have caught a taste of this enjoyment I want to simplify the externals of my life in order to enhance it, assuredly I will enjoy the means of life that helps me toward the end of my ultimate enjoyment. But as to whether simplicity is enjoyable in and for itself, the New Testament simply has no opinion; it does not deny the proposition; it just doesn't find the question relevant to the matter at hand. And so, if one does happen to discover for himself that the simple pleasures are best, fine; Jesus already had suggested that many other things would come to you as well. But what is certain is that a simple life motivated by the enjoyment of *God* will be much more satisfying and enduring than a fad that sees no further than the enjoyment of simple things in themselves.

Service to the Poor

This argument, heard frequently, takes two different approaches, either of which comes to pretty much the same thing. The one assumes that I have a level of income above what I actually need and that, by simplifying my life, I can free money that then can be devoted to helping the poor and other such worthy causes. The other approach assumes that I will bring my income down to a level that can be shared much more widely across the board, thus making a witness and contribution to the equalization of wealth. The one approach comes through most strongly on *philanthropy* and the second on *social justice and equality;* but there does not seem to be any particular conflict or competition between the two; they point very much in the same direction.

The first observation to be made is that this rationale is much more inherently Christian than is that of hedonism; there can be no denying that the New Testament displays a vital concern that one love, serve, and strive to ameliorate the conditions of the poor. Yet, even though this is a strong thrust in the teaching of Jesus, it is made in such a way as to indicate that he did not give it determinative, overriding priority.

For instance, Jesus' counsel to the rich, young ruler is, "Go, sell everything you have, and give to the poor, and you will have riches in heaven; and come, follow me" (Mark 10:21). Yet the total context (including both the incident with the young man and Jesus' subsequent remarks to the disciples) and, indeed, even the wording of the counsel itself make it plain that Jesus' primary concern was not for the poor but for the spiritual condition of the young man himself. The "sell everything" is pointed much more strongly toward the "come, follow me" than toward the "give to the poor." The young man's possessions are obstructing his view of the stars and must be sloughed off in order to free him for God. However, once he chooses to make *that* move, the giving of those possessions to the poor would become a very good way of disposing of them.

Perhaps an even more pointed instance is this from Mark:

> *Jesus was at Bethany, in the house of Simon the leper. As he sat at table, a woman came in carrying a small bottle of very costly perfume, pure oil of nard. She broke it open and poured the oil over his head. Some of those present said to one another angrily, "Why this waste? The perfume might have been sold for thirty pounds and the money given to the poor"; and they turned upon her with fury. But Jesus said, "Let her alone. Why must you make trouble for her? It is a fine thing she has done for me. You have the poor among you always, and you can help them whenever you like; but you will not always have me."*
>
> — Mark 14:3-7

The onlookers come through on cue with the correct and pious expression of Christian social concern. But, surprisingly, Jesus refuses to accept this as being the first order of business; he will not criticize the woman either

for owning this expensive nonessential in the first place
or for the "wasteful" way in which she disposes it. Jesus
interprets her act as being an expression of love toward
himself (and thus, at the same time, a commitment of
loyalty to God); and he states quite explicitly that it is
proper for this to take priority over helping the poor.

A profound insight is involved at this point. Jesus' act
is not a jealous grab of honor and attention for himself,
nor is it in any way a slighting of the poor. It is a way of
saying that the poor themselves will receive more help if
God is made the center of loyalty than if the poor themselves were put into that slot.

I think it quite unlikely that very many people for very
long can be motivated to lower their own standard of
living solely out of a humanitarian concern over the plight
of the poor. Men, by nature, simply are not that altruistic
— no matter how beautifully they may discourse on the
topic. This truth was brought home to me with force
through a television interview that took place at the time
Sargent Shriver accepted the Democratic vice-presidential
nomination in 1972. Leading up to the interview itself, an
announcer recounted Shriver's background, emphasizing
particularly his leadership in the poverty program and
other service projects. While these words were being
heard, the cameras panned over the Shriver home and
grounds. What was most obvious was that, no matter how
much Shriver has done for the poor, one thing he has not
done is to let it constrict his own standard of living.

In telling this story I am not taking a cheap shot at
Shriver; the incident is significant precisely because he *is*
a man who puts most of us to shame in the truly humanitarian concern he has shown. So I say again that it is quite
unlikely that very many people for very long can be
motivated to lower their own standard of living solely

out of a humanitarian concern over the plight of the poor.

However, if one sets his mind on the kingdom of God before everything else, then some totally new factors are brought into play. Now, out of his fascination with the stars, the person already is inclined to dispose of a bunch of his lanterns; and Jesus' suggestion to the rich, young ruler still holds: giving them to the poor is a fine thing to do with superfluous lanterns. Further, the person's very relationship to God *includes* the motivation, guidance, and *enablement* for his loving and serving the poorer brethren. So the poor themselves should be the first to applaud the fact that Jesus accepted the perfume for himself rather than giving it to them; his act was the best possible guarantee of their receiving what they need.

Yes, social justice, equality, and help for the poor are involved in the simple life; yet keep them where they belong, not as its motive and rationale, but as a "plus," a gift, a freedom, a grace out of the "all the rest" that will come to you as well.

Ecology

Today an urgent new rationale for simple living has obtruded upon us. Unless we voluntarily discipline our present runaway rate of consumption, we shortly will bring disaster upon the race either through the contamination of our environment, through the depletion of essential natural resources or, most likely, through both at once.

Now the best analysis of the facts seems clearly to indicate that our description of the threat is accurate. The logic of what must be done is unimpeachable. Every rational consideration would indicate that this matter of survival should constitute the one most immediate and compelling motivation for simple living that could be offered.

Logically it *should;* practically, I am convinced that it does not. Why it does not is a little hard to say: partly, perhaps, because fear is not a motive to which people respond very well. Partly because men never have done too well at sacrificing present pleasure for the sake of any future advantage — the actuality of the accessible present too much overweighs the elusive possibilities of a remote future. And partly because of a weird perversity that moves men to act contrary to their own best interests just to prove that they don't *have* to be compelled by logic.

A contemporary social experience most strongly impels me to this conclusion. Established even more scientifically and certainly than the prediction of environmental disease and death is the diagnosis that smoking is a direct cause of individual disease and death. The threat in this instance not only is more certain, more closely linked to present activity, and more immediate and selective in its repercussions than is the environmental threat, but, as well, the removal of the smoking threat could be accomplished with very much less of personal sacrifice — merely through a giving up of the foul stuff. And yet people simply will *not* quit smoking.

Now this perversity is at least somewhat understandable (and worthy of sympathy) in those who are caught in an addiction that will power is just incompetent to break. But the chilling thing is to watch our youth — the age group that is most knowledgeable about the effects of smoking, that is not impelled by the force of already-established addiction, and that we have touted as having the superior moral sensitivity that is the hope of saving our environment — how chilling it is to watch them keep total cigarette sales climbing even while older smokers are quitting the habit at a rate that otherwise would bring them downward.

And what makes the situation even more difficult regarding the environmental crisis is that very many people will need to act before the action has any effect on the problem at all. Thus, if I look around and do not see that anyone else is hurting himself to save the situation, I draw the natural conclusion that it would be stupid for me to give up my piece of the pie to no purpose at all.

But if commanding self-interest can't lead us even to give up a noisome weed, what possible chance is there that, before we are *forced* to do so, it will lead us voluntarily to cut back on our oh-so-enjoyable consumption of "the necessities of life"?

And yet, in regard to our secular society, there is no alternative but to keep preaching the not-too-effective gospel of self-interest and to hope beyond hope that somehow people will wake up and do something. Christians, however, don't have to be stuck in this boat. They have a rationale for the simple life that is infinitely superior to mere self-interest. And even more to the point, they have a gospel that goes far beyond man's saving himself by pulling at his own ecological bootstraps; it includes a God who can and will straighten out perversities and give men what it takes to discipline their rate of consumption, first of all as a way of getting themselves correctly positioned to enjoy this God, and then — as an entirely free bonus — as an effective way of meeting the environmental crisis as well.

And if this is the way it is with the *Christian* doctrine of the simple life, how tragic it would be if we were to trade it in for the ecological doctrine of sheer self-interest. And yet this is precisely what is happening in our churches. I would wager that from our pulpits there are to be heard ten appeals to ecological threat for every appeal to Christian simplicity. Yet the ecologists themselves should be the first to applaud the fact that Jesus asks for loyalty to himself even before loyalty to the environment; his demand is the best possible guarantee that the environment will get what it needs.

Asceticism

Here we encounter a mode of thought and life that often is confused with the Christian simple life but actually has no part in it. Asceticism starts from an assumption that came into Christian thought not from its native Hebrew tradition but from other cultures with which it came in contact. In point of fact, it is in complete contradiction to the biblical presupposition.

This foreign assumption is that there are two different and opposed worlds. The one is the world of stuff and things, the materiality amidst which we live our everyday lives. But over against this there stands an invisible, immaterial, ideal, "spiritual" world. Now it is this spiritual world that is the proper home of God and thus the locus of all that is good and true and beautiful. Conversely, the material world — precisely because it is constituted of material rather than spirit — is evil, is in itself a sign of fallenness and corruption.

According to the thinking of asceticism, then, one becomes saved by basing his existence as much as possible in the realm of spirit and as little as possible in the realm of materiality. And thus the ascetic ideal has been to own little or nothing, eat and drink and wear as little as possible, contemplate earthly realities as seldom as necessary.

Now this mode of thought has a certain superficial and

misleading likeness to the Christian simple life in its insistence that authentic personal existence must center in what it would call "spiritual reality" and we have called "an inner relationship of loyalty to God." But the basic conception behind these two ideas is quite different, because biblical thought is insistent that there is but *one* world — one world created *good* by a good God, created good in both its material and immaterial aspects; and these aspects are so completely amalgamated as to be entirely inseparable, let alone one capable of being judged superior to the other.

Here there is no suggestion of a world that is evil by virtue of its nature and origin. Biblically speaking, evil arises only as the perversion of the one world that was created and is intrinsically good, the distortion of people and things that were created and are intrinsically good. Indeed, so committed is the Bible to this view that it will not picture salvation in terms of material flesh going to extinction while a spiritual (and consequently good) soul enjoys its immortality in the spirit world. No, the biblical picture consistently is that of a total bodily-spiritual person resurrected to live upon a resurrected and redeemed earth.

The Christian simple life is not in any sense an attempt to suppress or deny the material side of human existence. Stuff and things are *good,* recognized as good gifts created by a good God for good purposes. They become bad only when man turns them to bad purposes. Better said: they do not become bad at all; rather, man allows the good of these gifts *from* God to obscure the greater good of enjoying God himself. Somewhere in every person's life there is a point of balance that can capture the best from both of these "goods." Finding that point won't be easy; but it is what we are after. However, once the man himself gets

right with God, "things" can become good in every respect
by finding their proper place within this triangular God-
man-things relationship. Asceticism, on the other hand,
cannot affirm that there is any good place for stuff and
things.

We need to be aware, too, of a second form of asceticism,
very similar to and compatible with the first and yet
reached by a slightly different route — although one just
as false as that of the first. This way of thinking does not
so much stress the inherent evil of materiality as it does
the meritoriousness of self-deprivation — obviously a second side of the same coin. But now, to the degree that I
punish my material self, to that degree I have earned
spiritual credits with God.

In this respect, confusion with the Christian idea of the
simple life arises from the fact that Jesus speaks much of
self-denial, of giving up everything in order to follow him.
Yet the economy is entirely different in the two cases. Jesus
nowhere talks in terms of deliberately hurting oneself in
an attempt to trade earthly pain for heavenly pleasure. No,
for Jesus, self-denial is more like a swimmer getting rid of
his outer clothing in order truly to enjoy his swimming.
And the Christian rids himself of his excess possessions,
not because they are bad in themselves or because he feels
it somehow good (or a way to impress the coach) for him
to freeze himself, but because getting stripped is the very
thing he most *wants* to do in order to get the full effect
of a glorious plunge into the cool pool and still waters of
God (or, to put it otherwise, a view of the stars).

However, the clearest proof that the simple life is not
asceticism is Jesus' own example and the obvious contrast
between himself and a true ascetic, John the Baptist. The
difference even got Jesus into trouble for not being as
"holy" as people thought he ought to be.

> *For John came, neither eating nor drinking, and they*
> *say, "He is possessed." The Son of Man came eating and*
> *drinking, and they say, "Look at him! a glutton and a*
> *drinker, a friend of tax-gatherers and sinners!"*
>   — Matthew 11:18-19

The simple life and the ascetic life are not the same; in this case the contrast was conspicuous to the eyes of beholders. But this means that the simple life is not nearly as easy to spot and identify by its outward markings as is the ascetic renunciation of material reality. Indeed, in at least some aspects, the simple life must be well-nigh invisible — if Jesus can be accused of being a glutton and drinker. And right here is the difficulty: to the extent that the simple life is outwardly ambiguous, to that extent it also is very easy to fake. And so, with Jesus, we must insist upon the presence of its inner reality rather than upon prescribed appearances of outward form. Otherwise, John the Baptist rather than Jesus becomes the model of the simple life.

Now in the sensate and materialistic culture that is ours, asceticism would not appear to be a particular threat — until we realize that we may be witnessing the resurgence of new forms of asceticism, precisely in reaction to our sensate and materialistic culture.

Rather apparent currents of ascetic thought and practice run through the Eastern religions and cults that in our midst are both winning out-and-out converts and influencing those who still consider themselves Christians. Some people, I understand, actually have broken their health through the ascetic diet by which they attempted to become "spiritual."

There is evidence that the earthly-pain-buys-heavenly-glory type of asceticism may be infecting certain sectors of the Jesus Movement.

And, interestingly enough, at least one psychologist claims to have spotted a variant form of asceticism in the current "organic foods" fad. He thinks that many young people who follow this enthusiasm are all unconsciously trying to achieve their own moral and spiritual purification by taking in only "pure" foods.

But whatever the situation, the Christian response to our thing-sick culture is the simple life and not any form of asceticism. Yet we need to be aware of the current trend, knowledgeable about the distinction, and alert to the dangers of confusion. And the one protection is to set one's mind on the kingdom of God before everything else, and *let* the "all the rest" come to you as well.

Dissociation from Society

In addition to the above, there is a somewhat different form of asceticism that, for many people, is now threatening to displace Christianity's simple life. It is a concern serious enough that we will devote an entire chapter to it a bit later. Here we will spend only enough time to get it on our list and relate it to a couple of the sayings of Jesus.

In this instance it is not the material world that is renounced as being totally evil; it is the *societal* world — and in particular the contemporary social establishment in which the person finds himself. For the most part, this social asceticism does not represent a carefully developed philosophy such as lies behind classic ascetic thought; it marks much more of a spontaneous, gut-level rebellion against a hypocritical and oppressive social regime.

Nevertheless, "the simple life" now becomes a life style designed expressly to demonstrate that the practitioner is no part of and wants nothing to do with established society. Even very minor details of dress and personal habit take on prime significance as symbols of a distancing oneself from the dominant culture.

Now, in striving to relate all of this to the teaching of Jesus, the first thing to be said is that, if one truly sets his mind on the kingdom of God before everything else, properly and inevitably this should create a distinction between his way of life and that of a world that is oriented to totally different values. The societal ascetics are right thus far (if, indeed, they have come thus far, that is, to a primary loyalty to the kingdom of God) ; such a loyalty and a distinction from the world are inevitable correlates.

However, as soon as one lets his single focus slip across from the kingdom of God and onto this distinction from the world, then he has botched the Christian succession. Just because commitment to the kingdom involves a distinction from the world, it does not follow that any and every distinction from the world automatically qualifies as commitment to the kingdom. The order of priority cannot be reversed; and the Christian simple life always is a positive doctrine of the enjoyment of God before it is a negative doctrine concerning the evil of the world. Protest against and challenge to the way of the world certainly has its proper place in the Christian economy; but that place must be with the "all the rest" that comes as well rather than with the "before everything else."

That Jesus himself did not make conspicuous dissociation from society a prime objective of his ministry is indicated by what we know of his personal demeanor. As we already have seen, he was willing to participate in society in such a way that at least opened him to the charge of being a glutton and drunkard — and a friend of tax-gatherers (who are nothing if not establishment types!) .

But more to the point, the Gospel records would indicate
that he was not adverse to being seen in and even attending
banquets in the homes of society's upper crust; that he did
in fact circulate as freely in the social establishment as
among the social outcasts; and that he showed no particular concern to make sure that no one mistakenly
identified him with the establishment crowd. He would
have felt just as free to mix and be mixed with the people
inside the Miami Beach Convention Center as with those
in Flamingo Park on the outside — and he would have felt
just as free to mount a critique against one group as
against the other.

Very relevant to this point is Jesus' response to the question of paying taxes: "Pay Caesar what is due to Caesar,
and pay God what is due to God" (Mark 12:17). Now the
interpretation proposed by many expositors can be quickly
granted: Jesus is not at all suggesting that the pie be split
fifty-fifty between God and Caesar; rather, the case is,
"Give God the kind of ultimate loyalty that belongs to
him and give Caesar the pennies that bear his image."
Nevertheless, neither can that saying be twisted to say,
"Give God everything, and to hell with Caesar." If Jesus
had meant that, he would have said so.

Certainly, the "before everything else" constitutes God's
share, and it is out of the "all the rest" that Caesar's share
must come; but the simple life *cannot* be motivated by a
sheer denial of connection with Caesar and the societal
world he represents. Obviously, what we have here is a
dialectic relationship; we will set up that dialectic and
juggle it a little in a chapter to come.

The present chapter has borne down hard upon one's
inner stance toward God as being constitutive for the
simple life; our scripture sources would not allow us to

write it any other way. Yet, although we have not been at all specific as to what the outward manifestations of the simple life look like, implications about the *necessity* of there *being* outward manifestations have been present all the way through. I trust they have not been lost upon (or evaded by) the reader. But if one were to give his loyalty completely to God's kingly rule and then discover that this required no change either in his attitude toward the things of the world or in the way he actually conducts himself regarding them, then obviously God doesn't amount to very much and commitment to him is no big deal. It is the case, then, that, in the simple-life dialectic, if the pole of outward manifestation is slighted, this necessarily will mark a subversion of the primary, before-everything-else pole as well. Although there is difficulty in giving it detailed emphasis and description, this secondary pole is just as essential as the primary one. Please don't read this book so as to disparage it.

Chapter Three

AS YOU WERE

"Liberation" is the catchword of our day; so let's talk about liberation. We didn't do it in the previous chapter, but we could as well have cast Jesus' teachings regarding the simple life into liberationist terminology. Clearly, the simple-living Christian dispossesses himself of excess stuff precisely that he might be *liberated* from it and so left free to enjoy the view of the stars, to live out of his love and loyalty to God.

In a crucial passage from a letter to the Corinthians, the Apostle Paul speaks very directly to the matter of liberation — although his remarks touch the simple life only tangentially. However, it will be easy enough to discover the implication his thought has for our particular topic.

Let us get the text before us:

Each one must order his life according to the gift the Lord has granted him and his condition when God called him. That is what I teach in all our congregations. Was a man called with the marks of circumcision on him? Let him not remove them. Was he uncircumcised when he was called? Let him not be circumcised. Circumcision is neither here nor there; what matters is to keep God's commands. Every man should remain in the condition in which he was called. Were you a slave when

*you were called? Do not let that trouble you; but if a
chance of liberty should come, take it. For the man who
as a slave received the call to be a Christian is the Lord's
freedman, and, equally, the free man who received the
call is a slave in the service of Christ. You were bought
at a price; do not become slaves of men. Thus each one,
my friends, is to remain before God in the condition in
which he received his call. . . .*

*What I mean, my friends, is this. The time we live in
will not last long. While it lasts, married men should
be as if they had no wives; mourners should be as if they
had nothing to grieve them, the joyful as if they did not
rejoice; buyers must not count on keeping what they buy,
nor those who use the world's wealth on using it to the
full. For the whole frame of this world is passing away.*

*I want you to be free from anxious care. . . . In saying
this I have no wish to keep you on a tight rein. I am
thinking simply of your own good, of what is seemly,
and of your freedom to wait upon the Lord without
distraction.* — 1 Corinthians 7:17-35

There is one consideration that must be dealt with at
the outset in order even to establish the validity of our
using this passage. Clearly, one of the governing factors in
Paul's thought is his expectation that "the time we live in
will not last long," that "the whole frame of this world is
passing away," that attention to the imminent, in-breaking
consummation of history (the eschaton) should figure
large in our ethical decisions.

Now the fact that more than nineteen hundred years
have elapsed while the world has gone its "merry" way
would seem to indicate that Paul's expectation was misplaced. Many commentators move, then, to the conclusion
that, because the expectation was misplaced, Paul's ethical
thought based upon that expectation is itself rendered in-
valid. Because he thought the time was short, he argued
that the matter of getting a change in earthly conditions

and alignments was of relatively low priority; but, because *we* know that the time is not short, the matter of earthly amelioration becomes of top priority.

However, this interpretation needs to be challenged on several levels. In the first place, even if, for the moment, we grant such a reading of Paul, it does not follow that we now know that the time is not short. The fact that the eschaton did not happen *then* gives us no information one way or the other as to whether it will happen *now*. Paul's attitude of expectation is just as possible and just as justified for us as it was for him.

But the heart of the matter lies at a somewhat different spot. Paul's expectations of imminence were *not* founded upon any claim of inside information as to *when* the eschaton would occur. Neither he nor other New Testament writers claimed to be one up on Jesus in this regard. For one thing, time after time throughout the Gospels, Jesus is reported as warning people against trying to discover "signs" and decipher them (Matt. 12:38-40; 16:1-4; Mark 8:11-13; 13:5-6, 21-23; Luke 11:29-30; 17:20-25; 21:7-8; John 21:20-23; Acts 1:6-8) . Yet *knowledge* about the "when" inevitably will have to involve the reading of signs — which Jesus himself warns is a very risky and deceptive business at best. More, Jesus explicitly denied that *he* had any such information: "But about that day and hour no one knows, not even the angels in heaven, not even the Son; only the Father" (Matt. 24:36) . And if Jesus denied that he did, who would be so presumptuous as to claim that he *does?*

And yet Jesus, like Paul, did have a very lively *expectation* of the end. However, that expectation was founded not upon any inside information about the "when" but precisely upon the *lack* of such information: the fact that I have not the slightest *knowledge* of "when" means that it could be at any time, as well now as a thousand years from now.

The crucial, summary statement in Matthew 24 makes it very clear that this was the nature of the early Christian expectation:

> *Keep awake, then; for you do not know on what day your Lord is to come. Remember, if the householder had known at what time of night the burglar was coming, he would have kept awake and not have let his house be broken into. Hold yourselves ready, therefore, because the Son of Man will come at the time you least expect him.*
>
> — Matthew 24:42-44

It is interesting to note, then, that, in the collection of parables that follow this text and illustrate it, the first (that of the untrustworthy servant) is the story of a man who got in trouble because he assumed that his master would return *late* when, in fact, he came *early*. But the next two (the wise and foolish maidens and the story of the talents) deal with people who are embarrassed because they assumed that the master (bridegroom) would come *early* when, in fact, he came *late*. The Christian expectation is one that can handle either eventuality, precisely because it does not claim to know when and thus can and will *continue* to be expectant no matter what happens. The fact that I don't *know* when always means that it *could* be *now*.

Thus, there is all the difference in the world between an expectation based upon a claim to inside information with its reading of the signs and an expectation based expressly upon the lack of any such information. The first is completely vulnerable to disappointment: "I was sure I knew when it was to happen; it didn't; I was all wrong."

However, the second is immune to this sort of disappointment: "Yes, I have been expecting the event; true, it
hasn't happened *yet;* but that doesn't mean I was 'wrong,'
because I never claimed to know when it would happen;
that it could be 'now' is still just as possible as it ever was."

Many New Testament scholars like to talk about "the
delay of the eschaton" and how it caused a major crisis in
the expectations of the early church and thus a radical
theological readjustment. I confess that the evidence im-
presses me precisely the other way. The Gospel records
indicate that Jesus (*circa* A.D. 30) held a very immediate
expectation of the end. At least twenty years later, Paul
(as per the selection before us) entertains just as lively an
expectation. As much as fifty years after Jesus, the Gospel
writers (particularly Matthew) must have shared the same
expectancy òr else they would have glossed over this aspect
of Jesus' teaching rather than emphasizing it. And, I
would maintain, the book of Revelation (whenever it was
written) displays as strongly as ever this same sort of I-
don't-*know*-when expectancy rather than making a claim
to privileged chronological information. It is almost incredible that an expectancy of the latter sort could maintain itself in force for a half-century and more; too many
people too often would have been proved all wrong.

And on the other hand, if there is evidence of theological modification occasioned by the delay of the eschaton, I submit that it should be understood not as a wise
and proper adjustment necessitated by a growing insight
into reality but rather as nothing more than a deteriora-
tion of faith. There is no reason at all why Christians today
cannot and should not share completely in Paul's sense of
eschatological expectancy and thus grant full validity to
the ethical argument he presents here.

(The modern church, however, has really missed the

point in this regard. It is divided into two camps. The
ultra-conservative literalists are correct in holding a lively
sense of eschatological expectancy, but they corrupt and
falsify that faith by basing it upon claims of inside information, an uninhibited passion for "signs," and the making
of the Bible into a code book. Thus they are courting
the very disillusionment Jesus warned against. The rest
of the church, on the other hand, is correct in understanding that God purposely is reserving the "when" of
the kingdom to his own secret wisdom; but these people
then jump to the completely unwarranted conclusion that
eschatology is irrelevant to the Christian faith and life.
And the biblical truth of the matter falls right through
the gap between these two faulty viewpoints.)

Nevertheless, New Testament ethics in general — and
thus the doctrine of the simple life in particular — are
governed by eschatological tension. This is the case even
where the expectation is not stated—although it very often
is. Thus, for example, it would be proper to read invisible
words into our key statement from Jesus: "Set your mind
on God's kingdom before everything else, [for that kingdom is fast approaching its consummation,] and all the
rest will come to you as well." When Paul points up the
eschatological orientation of our thought, he is not adding
anything new to the teaching of Jesus but simply making
more explicit what had been there all along.

But what is essential now is to discover *how* Paul uses
this eschatological expectancy, what role it plays in and
what contribution it makes to his ethical formulation.
It would seem, in the first place, that his expectancy does
not change the *content* of the ethic, that is, it does not
make anything right that otherwise would be wrong or
make wrong what otherwise would be right. What it does
do is sharpen and clarify *priorities*.

The economy is this: Let us say that there are two things that need to be done — No. 1 and No. 2 — each of them good and proper in themselves. Now, if time is no factor — and particularly if No. 2 seems to be the easier and more immediately manageable task — the tendency is to say, "Let's give No. 2 the big push now, and we can get around to No. 1 in due course." If, however, eschatological expectancy makes it very much a possibility that time may be limited, the word is, "We had better make sure that No. 1 is getting the primary attention before we give too much concern to No. 2."

On the face of it, the matter of ordering priorities would seem to be minor enough; but as we saw in the previous chapter and as we shall see now in regard to a somewhat different dialectic, there are at least some situations in which the order of priority is all-important. It is as with a radio set: it is not enough that it simply contain the proper components; unless those components are hooked up in proper order, properly related to one another, the set will not operate at all.

Thus, in one sense, his eschatological expectancy adds no new component to Paul's ethical analysis. What he says would be true in any case: No. 1, because it is in fact more important than No. 2, *should* get priority whether that is the way things turn out or not. But the very vital contribution the eschatological expectancy makes, then, is as guide and insurance that the true priorities *will* be recognized and ordered in such a way that the system as a whole can operate.

Now Paul's is a system of *liberation;* this is his topic throughout the passage. He suggests that there are two different modes of liberation or, better, two different components that belong in the system. These form a dialectic; and yet (as in the instance of the previous chapter) it is crucial that the proper priority between the poles be observed.

No. 1 is an inner attitude toward external circumstances by which one can free himself from them even before the circumstances themselves are changed, even if they do not come to be changed. No. 2 is the changing of the external circumstances themselves.

Certainly it will not require more than a second's consideration to realize that all of the liberation movements that characterize our society today devote their single and exclusive attention to No. 2. No. 1 is positively disdained — if its possibility is even recognized. Thus Paul's order of priority is entirely reversed (and undoubtedly the reason Paul wrote as he did was because, in his own day, some Corinthians were intent on making the same inversion).

But consider the consequences. That the focus of liberation now centers upon the external situation of oppression means, in fact, that it centers upon the external *people* whom I see as having created the situation, "the male chauvinist pigs," or whoever. An "adversary" alignment is created; and the picture immediately becomes that of a righteous, innocent, but misused "me" fighting myself free from the oppressive evil of the black-hearted "them." Of course, there also may be pious talk about the fact that we are getting free in order to free them as well; but neither the rhetoric nor the action can maintain that spirit or remain convincing on that point for very long.

The promise of liberation now becomes an invitation for me to ferret out and worry over every conceivable slight and inequity in my effort to convince the world how misused I am — this is called "the raising of awareness." And the motive power behind the movement thus becomes my offendedness and moral indignation, it becomes hurt, anger, resentment, rebellion — building precisely upon the "anxious care" from which Paul wishes to set us free. And there is something wrong with an effort that fosters the very thing from which it is striving to be liberated.

It is telling in this regard that one of the counsels Paul gives his readers is, "Do not become slaves of men" — this to people who, above all, are determined to fight themselves free from the men who *have* enslaved them. Obviously, Paul intends something different from the meaning they would attach to those words. He is saying, is he not?: "Be careful or in your very efforts at liberation you will let men enslave you into bitterness and lack of love. You are going after Liberation No. 2 exactly in a way that will lose you Liberation No. 1. What a tragedy!"

Now I do not believe that Paul means to eliminate entirely the effort to change external conditions or to suggest that such efforts are of no importance — although, because the Corinthian imbalance was so far the other way, he does come close to doing it, I admit. Nevertheless he does counsel the slave that "if a chance of liberty should come, take it." And I am confident that he also would want to say, "If a chance should come of helping some other slave be liberated, take it even more quickly." So Paul's real meaning seems to be that the finding and sharing of the inner freedom that rises above external circumstances takes priority and is the Christian's first order of business. But then, as opportunity presents itself — *and if God should grant us time* — it is altogether right to work at bringing about outward change as well. (And the so-called "delay of the eschaton" does mean this much if nothing else: to the present, at least, God *has* granted us time. Paul's doctrine offers no comfort to contemporary Christians who have done a miserable enough job of No. 1, to be sure, but who haven't got around to No. 2 either.)

But in this thought of Paul there also lies the explana-

tion of a behavior that often has raised questions. Paul
and the other early Christians (and Jesus himself) lived in
a society that practiced human slavery . . . and yet they
made no apparent effort either to change, challenge, or
even protest the situation. Why not? Because, in the short-
ness of the time of eschatological expectation, they were
concerned, urgently concerned, to get to every slave (i.e.,
every *person*) that quality of liberation that makes bodily
release seem comparatively unimportant. "For the man
who as a slave received the call to be a Christian is the
Lord's freedman, and, equally, the free man who received
the call is a slave in the service of Christ." Then, if it
pleases God to grant us time (as it turns out he did), we
can work at changing the social institution of external
slavery as well.

There would seem to be a further consideration Paul
did not raise but we will volunteer to raise for him. A
person who already has found Liberation No. 1 is bound
to be much more effective in gaining Liberation No. 2
both for himself and for others than will the person who
tries directly for No. 2. The old One-Two (in that order)
Punch avoids all the side effects of suspicion, accusation,
and bitterness that we observed in the other approach.
And so we reiterate an earlier formula: by rights, the
liberationists should be the first to applaud when a person
chooses to follow the Pauline priority rather than straight-
way joining the Movement; it is the best possible guarantee that the ends of the Movement will themselves
be realized.

Paul puts his primary emphasis on the No. 1 Liberation
that rises above circumstance, and it is this we want to be
most careful to understand. Paul's personal experience is
a very instructive example. His comparative de-emphasis

of the importance of social change was not motivated by the fact that he was a well-to-do WASP male (he could have qualified on only one of those counts) who never knew what oppression was. He was, rather, an indigent social and ethnic outcast who spent more time behind bars and was more often hassled by the establishment than is the case with ninety-nine percent of the people for whom liberation is being sought today. And yet, while sitting in a jail on a bum rap, he could write:

> *Not that I am alluding to want, for I have learned to find resources in myself whatever my circumstances. I know what it is to be brought low, and I know what it is to have plenty. I have been very thoroughly initiated into the human lot with all its ups and downs — fullness and hunger, plenty and want. I have strength for anything through him who gives me power.*
>
>   — Philippians 4:11-13

The man who wrote that knows a liberation that goes deeper than anything the modern movement has dreamed of. And, consequently, Paul's writings show a marked absence of complaint, demand, rant, rancor, and sneer; he is free enough from his oppressors that he does not have to allow them to dictate the mood of his existence.

On one occasion (Acts 16:25ff.) Paul and his companions were in prison when God acted through an earthquake to change the external circumstances and grant them a No. 2 type liberation. They declined to leave their cells. And why? Because to do so would get the jailer into trouble. When people can afford to take such an attitude, so diametrically contrary to what characterizes much of modern liberationism, it is proof enough that they already have experienced an infinitely higher quality of liberation. However, it must be said, too, that action of this caliber never can come about by trying to *make* people

stay in their cells or by preaching at them that this is what
they *should* do. Only those who have experienced Liberation No. 1 are free enough to act so; and then they do it
because they *want* to.

But perhaps our most telling example comes from Jesus
rather than Paul. Recounted in Matthew 17:24-27, it has
to do with whether Jesus is obligated to pay the temple
tax. Jesus' first response is that such a tax cannot rightfully
be claimed from him; to impose it upon him is an in-
justice. Nevertheless, precisely because he is free and has
the liberty in this regard, he *chooses* to express it *by voluntarily paying the tax* because "we do not want to cause
offense." This willingness to *suffer* offense rather than
offend others by demanding that they give attention to *my*
offendedness again is the mark of a quality of liberation
that is altogether different from what the Movement
knows. But recall, too, what we suggested above, that the
cause of external amelioration itself will be better
served by this attitude of Jesus than by that of those
who are ready to try anything in the effort to throw off
the oppressor.

This is what Liberation No. 1 looks like; but what is its
source and economy? There is one sentence in our Paul
passage that speaks to the topic: "What matters is to keep
God's commands." Now, at root, that idea is almost
identical with Jesus' "Set your mind on God's kingdom
before everything else"; but perhaps Paul expresses his
thought somewhat more felicitously at another point: "I
count everything [including external amelioration] sheer
loss, because all is far outweighed by the gain [the libera-
tion] of knowing Christ Jesus my Lord" (Phil. 3:8) . What
we here have called "Liberation No. 1" is simply the
personal consequence of the inner relationship to God
that we earlier called the "Before Everything Else."

We are supposed to be talking about the simple life and
are ready to do so again. We have taken a roundabout
way to get here, but it enables us to state directly what
now needs to be said. Although not mentioning specifically
that which has to do with the simple life, Paul's argument
is very near the mark even so. His "I want you to be free
from anxious care" parallels Jesus' "I bid you put away
anxious thoughts." However, the difference in wording
may be significant. The most Paul can do is to express his
hope and desire that his reader *will* be freed from anxious
care; but only Jesus has the authority and power to com-
mand, "I *bid* you," and then grant what he commands.

But as regards "the things of life," anxious care indicates
that one is *enslaved* by them. When a person's lanterns
keep him from enjoying the view of the stars, they have
deprived him of a precious liberty. And I think it hardly
is necessary for me to write anything aimed to convince the
reader that masses of our contemporaries have become
trapped into the slave march of making money and spend-
ing it — production, consumption, luxury, keeping up
with the Joneses. We need a liberation movement here as
much as in any other aspect of life.

But Paul's argument would indicate that liberation
from this slavery is not to be won by a direct attack upon
the "things" in themselves, by a first-priority attempt to
modify the externals of one's style of life. No, the key to
liberty lies primarily in an inner change of attitude toward
these things. And this attitude Paul (in the middle paragraph of our 1 Corinthians text) characterizes with the
phrase "as if not." The man with many possessions is to
consider them as if he had them not; the man without
possessions is to consider that lack as if it did not exist. And
such an attitude does, in itself, free one from the tyranny of
"things" — even before any concrete change is made re-

garding the things themselves. And it goes without saying that the only action that can bring about this new, as-if-not attitude is "the expulsive power of a new affection." "I count everything sheer loss, because all is far outweighed by the gain of knowing Christ Jesus my Lord."

This means, then, that the degree of a person's liberation, the quality of his freedom from "things," cannot be gauged simply by looking at how many things he owns. For example, I am certain that there are people who have possessions of a price I could never dream of owning who nevertheless are further liberated from "things" than I am. Likewise, I am certain that there are many people who own far less than I do and yet have tasted nothing of the liberation of Christian simplicity. But even so, as soon as we have said this, it is incumbent upon us also to say that there are some things which to own — and more particularly, there is a way of owning things — which makes it apparent to even the most casual observer that the owner is in no way free of his possessions.

It is right, then, to urge that the experience of Liberation No. 1 not end with that but move on into the external changes of Liberation No. 2. Yes, an as-if-not attitude *can* free one from the tyranny of his possessions; nevertheless, possession is itself a snare continually set to jerk a person out of his freedom. The matter is very cogently put by Jesus in his conversation with the disciples following the encounter with the rich, young ruler.

It had become evident that that young man could not hold an as-if-not attitude and continue to own his wealth at the same time; so Jesus commanded him to rid himself of it. Then . . .

> *Jesus looked round at his disciples and said to them, "How hard it will be for the wealthy to enter the kingdom of God!" They were amazed that he should say this,*

but Jesus insisted, "Children, how hard it is to enter
the kingdom of God! It is easier for a camel to pass
through the eye of a needle than for a rich man to enter
the kingdom of God." They were more astonished than
ever, and said to one another, "Then who can be saved?"
Jesus looked at them and said, "For men it is impossible,
but not for God; everything is possible for God."
                                              — Mark 10:23-27

Now the disciples were operating under the old Jewish
understanding that saw wealth entirely as a sign of God's
approval and blessing (a view regarding which many
Christians still have not caught on that Jesus rejected and
even reversed it) ; they simply had never thought of
wealth as a trap and enslavement. They were flabbergasted,
then, when Jesus turned their conception upside down by
stating that it is easier for a camel to pass through the
eye of a needle than for a rich man to enter the kingdom
of God.

For most of us, certainly, the indicated response to
Jesus' observation is that wealth is something we would
be smart to get rid of, choose not to seek, and be happy to
do without. And yet he does not say — he specifically does
not say — that every wealthy man automatically is dis-
qualified from entering the kingdom of God. No, when he
says that everything is possible for God, he can mean
nothing else than that some people *will* be able to find
the true Christian liberty of "as if not," even without
actually divesting themselves of what they happen to
possess.

Absolutely forbidden, then, is any tendency on our part
to look at what a person owns and so make a judgment regarding his spiritual state. Absolutely prescribed, on the
other hand, is the way to liberation and true Christian
simplicity. These *must* start with the inner matters of

relationship and attitude rather than with any external changes regarding "things." Granted, this setup leaves the field wide open for us sinners to deceive either ourselves, other people, or both. And that is why, in the final analysis, the whole matter of Christian simplicity will have to be left in the hands of God — which is precisely where it belongs anyhow.

Chapter Four

IN BUT NOT OF

Earlier we suggested that the Christian concept of the simple life cannot be equated directly with sheer rejection of the prevailing social order. We saw that neither Jesus' teachings nor his example could be forced into so simplistic a pattern. Yet certainly, both for Jesus and for us, the simple life *does* entail elements of a witness against the world and its ways. The matter will need to be made *dialectical.*

It is this particular dialectic we propose to develop now. We already have noted some New Testament texts that deal with the subject, and we will bring in some others. However, what is perhaps the best early Christian statement comes not out of the New Testament itself but from a bit later in history, perhaps during the second century. Even so, all the indications are that this text is a fair representation of the New Testament's own teaching.

The document is a rare and little noted fragment of an early Christian apology known as *The Letter to Diognetus.* Very little if anything definite can be said about who wrote it, when, where, or how. And we will use it, then, not so much as the thought of a particular author but more as an almost accidental peek into the culture of the early Christians and their practice of the simple life.

Christians are not different from the rest of men in nationality, speech, or customs; they do not live in states of their own, nor do they use a special language, nor adopt a peculiar way of life. . . . Whether fortune has given them a home in a Greek or foreign city, they follow local custom in the matter of dress, food, and way of life; yet the character of the culture they reveal is marvelous and, it must be admitted, unusual. They live, each in his native land — but as though they were not really at home there. They share in all duties like citizens and suffer all hardships like strangers. Every foreign land is for them a fatherland and every fatherland a foreign land. They marry like the rest of men and beget children, but they do not abandon the babies that are born. They share a common board, but not a common bed. In the flesh as they are, they do not live according to the flesh. They dwell on earth, but they are citizens of heaven. They obey the laws that men make, but their lives are better than the laws. They love all men, but are persecuted by all. They are unknown, and yet they are condemned. They are put to death, yet are more alive than ever. They are paupers, but they make many rich. They lack all things, and yet in all things they abound.[2]

This passage is a beautiful example of dialectic, even if nothing else. The concluding lines specifically but also the tone of the whole make it plain that the style of these Christians was a simple one; their lives obviously were not centered upon material values. Regarding the relationship, then, between them and the society around them, it also is made plain that this style was obnoxious to those who observed it; they interpreted it as a threat to and a judgment against their own values. So much was this the case that we are told that the Christians actually were persecuted and killed in consequence.

---

[2] "The Letter to Diognetus," trans. by Gerald G. Walsh, in *The Fathers of the Church*, Vol. 1 (Catholic University of America Press, 1962), pp. 360-61.

Nevertheless (and here comes the dialectic), it also is made clear that the Christian style was not purposely designed to irritate other people or even willfully to demonstrate a difference and distance from them. Quite the contrary, we see these Christians making a deliberate effort to identify *with* the larger community; the entire first half of our passage points in this direction.

The normative principle behind their action seems to be this: except where their allegiance to Christ clearly dictates otherwise, they feel a real obligation to be identified with the people and affiliated with the culture in which they find themselves. Nonconformity is not valued as an end in itself. The one end is that which we have been emphasizing all the way through: loyalty to Jesus Christ and, through him, to the kingdom of God. Obviously, at points, this loyalty is going to show itself as nonconformity to the world; yet even there, the loyalty rather than the nonconformity is the motive and goal of the action. Absolutely no value is given here to nonconformity apart from such an act of loyalty.

Now, when the Christian, out of his loyalty to Jesus, does perform in a way that amounts to a rejection of the world's way, it is quite possible for the world (or at least some people in it) to see this as an exposé of its own evil and consequently be moved to a change of heart and of life. But it is *God's* business whether or not things do work out so; there is no evidence to suggest that Christian simplicity ever was meant *as a strategy* for protesting against the world or attempting to reform it. In a word, the validity of Christian simplicity is determined entirely by the good of that to which it *does* conform, namely, the kingdom of God, rather than by the evil of that to which it refuses to conform — even though God may choose to use that nonconformity as an injunction against evil. Or to put it again in the terms that form the true basis of our thought: "Set your mind on God's kingdom before everything else, and all the rest [including the condemnation and possible reformation of the world] will come to you as well."

From this analysis it should become apparent how different is the economy of *Christian* simplicity from the superficially similar simplicity of the contemporary counterculture. That movement, it seems quite apparent, is motivated almost exclusively by reaction, rebellion, protest, defiance *against* society, a society deemed to be essentially evil. Completely contrary to what we found in the Diognetus description, there now appears a conscious effort to discover and invent arbitrary symbols that can express and dramatize the stance of distancing and rejection. Whereas these early Christians were seeking out opportunities (Christianly permissible opportunities) for expressing their identity with their fellows of the larger society, the counterculture seeks out opportunities for expressing dissociation and contempt. Nonconformity is promoted as a good in and for itself.

Behind this difference, of course, lies the fundamental discrepancy that the counterculture lacks a positive center. Because it has nothing integral or true upon which to focus *in the positive,* it has to orient itself simply as protest *against the negative.* And as much of a positive witness as the counterculture can muster is the questionable assertion that simplicity is more sensuously satisfying than luxury is (see our earlier discussion of "hedonism").

It needs to be said that the counterculture's "rebellion toward simplicity" does have sociological significance and perhaps even a contribution to make in exposing the deep sickness of our sensate, materialistic, technique-dominated

society. But how disastrous it would be to confuse this
symptom of sickness with or equate it to that Christian
simplicity which is the *cure* of sickness — and that because
it points to and is controlled by the one who is himself
the Great Physician.

A second passage from Diognetus leads us into a theological analysis of the simplicity that the first passage
described.

> In a word, what the soul is to the body Christians are
> to the world. The soul is distributed in every member
> of the body, and Christians are scattered in every city in
> the world. The soul dwells in the body, and yet it is not
> of the body. So, Christians live in the world, but they are
> not of the world. The soul which is guarded in the
> visible body is not itself visible. And so, Christians who
> are in the world are known, but their worship remains
> unseen. The flesh hates the soul and acts like an unjust
> aggressor, because it is forbidden to indulge in pleasures.
> The world hates Christians — not that they have done it
> wrong, but because they oppose its pleasures. The soul
> loves the body and its members in spite of the hatred. So
> Christians love those who hate them. The soul is locked
> up in the body, yet it holds the body together. And so
> Christians are held in the world as in a prison, yet it is
> they who hold the world together.[3]

Now admittedly, this author's doctrine of the soul is
wide open to criticism — both on biblical grounds and on
the grounds of modern psychology and anthropology.
However, because neither he nor we have any interest in
discussing the soul as such, this need present no difficulty.
Our one concern will be to grasp his picture in order to
understand what he *is* talking about, the Christian's relationship to the world.

---

[3]*Ibid.*, p. 362.

He does not envisage the soul as many of us may, as an ethereal blob hidden somewhere within an individual; for him, the soul is an invisible, insubstantial body congruent with and contained within the person's material body. Further, the soul is by nature good and manifests a concern for the virtue and welfare of the person as a whole, whereas the physical body is interested only in its own sensual pleasure.

As before, the author's prime concern is to establish the *dialectic* character of the relationship he is exploring. He achieves his most succinct statement of it, perhaps, in the sentence: "So Christians live in the world, but they are not of the world." He did not invent this idea, although he may have been the first to put it just this tersely. But in the Gospel of John, Jesus' high-priestly prayer for his disciples includes each of the elements we have found here in Diognetus.

> *These things I speak in the world, that they may have my joy fulfilled in themselves. I have given them thy word; and the world has hated them because they are not of the world, even as I am not of the world. I do not pray that thou shouldst take them out of the world, but that thou shouldst keep them from the evil one. They are not of the world, even as I am not of the world. Sanctify them in the truth; thy word is truth. As thou didst send me into the world, so I have sent them into the world.*
> — John 17:13-18, RSV

This passage can help in interpreting and elaborating what the Diognetus author has said. He pointed us in the direction of giving the "*in*-the-world" pole of the dialectic proper attention along with the "*not-of*-the-world" pole. But Jesus makes it specific that his prayer is precisely *not* that his disciples should be taken out of the world. Yet, truly, the evidence suggests that what we have called "counterculture simplicity" *does* represent an attempt to get "out of the world" — no, not out of the *natural* world, of course, but out of the world of human society. The prevalence of drug use in this culture is perhaps the clearest indicator that this is the motivation involved.

But Jesus, too, is talking about the human world rather than the natural world; the final sentence of our John text makes that plain. To say that Christians are "in the world" implies much more than the simple-minded observation that in the world is where we happen to be and that we ought not try to fight the fact. Far from being merely an unavoidable fact of our existence, Jesus insists that Christians are "in the world" because he himself *sent* them into the world just as God sent *him* into the world. The Christian way of being in the world, then, is the way of conscious and deliberate religious commitment rather than the way of automatic and inevitable happenstance. And thus voluntary association in the world of men can be the only possible intention behind Jesus' words.

It goes without saying that God sent Jesus into the world for no other purpose than to love, serve, suffer with, and suffer for the men he found there. It follows indubitably that Christians are sent into the world with the same assignment. Now it obviously is impossible to communicate love and concern for one's fellow man unless one is willing, at the same time, to communicate the desire to understand, feel for, become involved and even identified with him. In that regard, Jesus' own ministry was so effective that the New Testament can say of him, "For we have not a high priest who is unable to sympathize with our weaknesses, but one who in every respect has been tempted as we are, yet without sinning" (Hebrews 4:15, RSV).

The calling of the Christian impels him to be working

every bit as hard at being *in* the world as at being *not of* it. In fact, just as soon as one of these tasks is disregarded, the other loses its validity at the same time. Many Christians have become so good at being *in* the world that there no longer is any evidence of their being *not of* it. That's worldliness; and that's *bad*. But the situation isn't helped when those of the counterculture overreact to that hypocrisy and become so scrupulous about being *not of* the world that they fail any longer to be *in* it. That's *self-righteous contemptuousness;* that's *bad,* too; and it is a hypocrisy of its own sort.

The Christian's not-of-the-world simplicity will offend people; both Jesus and the Diognetus author make this clear. Yet the Christian loves these very same people, knows that he is one of them, and wants to be known as one of them. Even though they find his action offensive, it is not that he wanted it to offend them; he was not out to "bug" them and takes no satisfaction in the fact that they got irritated.

In this regard, one of the most questionable assumptions behind the counterculture and its Christian camp following is the idea that one helps people by getting them riled up and pushed out of shape — or that any of us is wise and righteous enough to administer such therapy. Now if at times (as I fully believe is the case) a person's becoming offended does turn out to be the occasion for an achieving of new insight and his coming to repentance — still this is an outcome that had better be left in the hands of God. The Christian, it seems clear, is called to express his love of the neighbor in a more direct and unambiguous way — in a way that the neighbor himself will recognize as love.

Christians love those who hate them, and it is these Christians who *hold* the world together. This is what the Diognetus author tells us, rather than that they are those who work at tearing it apart in hopes of *getting* it all together. And so Christian simplicity must at all times be dialectical. And if its practitioner is to be *in* the world even while *not of* it, he must find the way to differ from the world without telling it to go to hell at the same time.

PART II

According to Kierkegaard

Chapter Five

SIMPLY PUT PARABLES

To the best of my knowledge, Søren Kierkegaard (Denmark, 1813-55) is the major thinker from Christian history who has given the most (and most effective) attention to the doctrine that we have been calling "the simple life." Such a claim must come as a shock to most people, scholars as well as laymen, because Kierkegaard generally is known as a sophisticated, super-intellectual philosopher, the father of Existentialism, a precursor of depth psychology, a theoretical aesthetician, and goodness knows what all — yet anything but a down-to-earth, Bible-believing Christian majoring in the simple life.

But the customary picture of Kierkegaard is wrong — although this is not the place to argue that matter through to a conclusion.[4] We shall see another side of Kierkegaard now; and it represents the man in his truest identity and in the witness he was most concerned to make. In that connection, we can note one tiny, but impressive, bit of evidence. An index has been compiled that catalogs the scripture references Kierkegaard used throughout his writings. From it, two things are readily apparent. First, Kierkegaard used the Bible a very great deal, referring to

---

[4]The place where I *have* done that is my earlier book, *Kierkegaard and Radical Discipleship* (Princeton University Press, 1968).

passages scattered from Genesis to Revelation and pausing frequently for more extended exposition. And second, rather clearly, out of all the texts to which he gave attention, the one that drew his most sustained and concentrated interest was Matthew 6:19-34, the very simple-life passage from the Sermon on the Mount we used as the basis of our second chapter.[5]

In a very real sense, then, the fact that our study now shifts from "According to Jesus and Company" to "According to Kierkegaard" does not represent any radical disjuncture at all. Our focus still is upon the New Testament teaching; it is only that we are inviting Kierkegaard to share with us *his* understanding of the matter.

One beauty of Kierkegaard's work is his skill in inventing parables that illuminate and drive home the point he wants to make. Several of his best center on our topic, the simple life. Let's look at them. (As we proceed, Kierkegaard's own words will appear in regular type and my commentary in italics.)

The Lighted Carriage and the Star-lit Night

We quoted and used this parable at the very outset of our book (see page 12 above), and it hardly is necessary to repeat it here. We should, however, remember to include it as perhaps the first of the parables of Kierkegaard.

Late for Church

This little story obviously does not get to the heart of what the simple life is all about; but it can help us realize how far we actually are from living that life.

---

[5]Minear and Morimoto, *Kierkegaard and the Bible: An Index* (Princeton Theological Seminary, 1953), p. 19.

Money, money — this is earnestness. So we are brought up, from earliest childhood, trained in ungodly money-worship. Permit me to cite an example, the first, the best among thousands and thousands — there are not more herring ahead of a boat working its way through a shoal of herring than there are examples of up-bringing in money-worship. Think of a household in which the head of the family recommends that on the next day (which is Sunday) all of them go to church together. But what happens? Sunday morning finds the girls not dressed in time. What does the father say then — earnest father, who earnestly brings up his children to worship money? Yes, he naturally says nothing, or as good as nothing, because there is no occasion here for a warning or a reprimand; he just says, "If the girls are not ready, we have to stay home; there is nothing else to do." But imagine, imagine how terrible it would be if the girls were to have gone to the theatre and they were not ready at the appointed time. How do you imagine this earnest father would carry on then, and why? Because in this case they had wasted considerable money; whereas by staying at home on Sunday they had saved at least the offering-money.[6]

The Anxious Lily and the Helpful Bird

This story takes off from Jesus' remark about the lilies of the field and the birds of the air and is a valid exposition of it. Even so, Kierkegaard's story is away out from the lilies and birds that Jesus was talking about.

There was once a lily that stood quite apart, near a little running brook, and was well acquainted with some nettles

---

[6]*Works of Love,* trans. by Howard and Edna Hong (Harper Torchbooks, 1964), pp. 296-97.

as well as a few other small flowers there in the neighbor-
hood. The lily was, according to the Gospel's veracious
description, more beautifully arrayed than Solomon in
all his glory, besides being carefree and happy the whole
day long. . . .

But it happened one day that a little bird came and
visited the lily; it came again the next day, and then it
remained away for several days before it came again;
which impressed the lily as being strange and inexplicable,
inexplicable that the bird should not stay in the same
place, like the small flowers — strange that the bird could
be so capricious. But as so often happens, so too it happened to the lily, that because the bird was so capricious,
the lily fell more and more in love with it.

This little bird was a bad bird; instead of putting itself
in the place of the lily, instead of rejoicing with it in its
beauty and innocent happiness, the bird wished to make
itself important by feeling its own freedom, and by making
the lily feel its bondage. And not only this, the little bird
was also talkative, and it would tell all kinds of stories,
true and false, about how there were, in other places, very
unusually magnificent lilies in great abundance; how there
were joy and gaiety, fragrance, brilliant coloring, a song
of birds, which far surpassed all description. . . .

So the lily became troubled; the more it listened to the
bird the more troubled it became. . . . Now it began to
occupy itself with itself and with the circumstances of its
life in its self-concern — so long was the day. . . . Said the
lily, "My wish is not an unreasonable desire; I do not ask
the impossible, to become what I am not, a bird, for example; my desire is only to become a splendid lily, or
even the most splendid one." . . .

At last it confided absolutely in the bird. One evening
they agreed that the next morning a change should take

place which would put an end to the concern. Early the next morning came the little bird; with its beak it cut the soil away from the lily's roots, so that it might thus become free. When this was accomplished, the bird took the lily under its wing and flew away. The intention was, of course, that the bird would take the lily to where the magnificent lilies bloomed; then the bird would again assist in getting it planted down there, to see if, through the change of soil and the new environment, the lily might not succeed in becoming a magnificent lily in company with the many, or possibly even an imperial lily, envied by all the others.

Alas, on the way the lily withered. If the discontented lily had been satisfied to be lily, then it would not have become concerned; if it had not become concerned, then it would have remained standing where it was — where it stood in all its beauty; had it remained standing, then it would have been precisely the lily about which the preacher spoke on Sunday, when he repeated the Gospel's words: "Consider the lily. . . . I say unto you that even Solomon in all his glory was not arrayed like it." . . .

And if a man, like the lily, is satisfied with the fact of being human, then he does not become ill from temporal concern; and if he does not become temporally concerned, then he continues to stand in the place appointed to him; and if he remains there, then it is truly so, that through being human he is more glorious than the glory of Solomon.[7]

Although that parable rightfully can be related to Jesus' "I bid you put away anxious thoughts about food and drink. . . ," its main thrust stands even closer to Paul's,

---

[7]*The Gospel of Suffering*, trans. by David and Lillian Swenson (Augsburg Publishing House, 1948), pp. 178-83.

*"Each one must order his life according to the gift the
Lord has granted him and his condition when God called
him."* Kierkegaard's story supports our critique of contemporary liberationist movements for defining liberation
solely in terms of changing one's external circumstances,
without any comprehension of that liberation which can
rise above circumstances without changing them.*

*Elsewhere, Kierkegaard makes the point even more tell-
ing, commenting directly upon Paul's text:*

Thus if one who is born a slave, in compliance with the
Apostle's heartfelt admonition (for Christ did not come
in order to abolish slavery, although this will follow and
will be a result of His coming) , he is not concerned about
it, and merely chooses freedom if it is offered: then he
bears the heavy burden lightly. How heavy this burden is,
the unhappy slave knows best, and human sympathy
understands it with him. If he groans under the burden,
as humanity groans with him, then he bears the burden
heavily. If he patiently submits to his fate, and patiently
hopes for freedom, then he still does not bear the burden
lightly. But the meek, who has had the courage really to
believe in spiritual freedom, bears the heavy burden
lightly: he neither relinquishes the hope of freedom, nor
does he expect it. The question which is rightly called
decisive, the question about freedom, the question which
for a slave-born individual may indeed be called a vital
question of being or not being: this mortal or life-giving
question the meek handles so easily, as if it did not concern him, and yet, in another way, so easily that in a way
it does concern him, for he says: "My being born a slave
does not concern me, but if I can become free, then would
I preferably choose that." To bite at the chain is to bear
it heavily, to ridicule the chain is also to bear it heavily;

patiently to endure the chain is still not bearing it lightly, but, slave-born, to bear the bond of slavery as a free man may carry a chain: that is bearing it lightly.[8]

The Wild Dove and the Tame

This story of the anxious bird is a twin of the parable of the anxious lily presented above. It, too, derives from Jesus' remark but, in this case, comes closer to what Jesus was actually emphasizing at that point, namely, that man can depend upon God's providence and thus need not be anxious in striving to construct security for himself out of his own resources.

There was once a stock-dove; in the grim forest, there where wonder also dwells with terror among the straight, solitary trunks, it had its nest. But near by, where the smoke arose from the farmer's chimney, there dwelt some of its more distant relations, some tame doves. It frequently met with a pair of these; that is, it sat on a branch overhanging the farmer's yard; the two tame doves sat on the ridge of the roof; however, the distance between them was not so great but that they could exchange thoughts with each other in conversation. . . .

The stock-dove said: "So far I have had my living; I let each day have its own worry and in that way I get through the world."

The tame doves had listened carefully. . . . Thereupon one answered: "Now we support ourselves differently; with us, that is to say, with the rich farmer with whom we live, one has his future assured. When harvest time comes, then one of us, I or my mate, sits up on the roof and

8*Ibid.,* pp. 36-37.

watches. Then the farmer drives one load of grain after another into the barn, and when he has driven so many in that I can no longer keep count, then I know that there are supplies enough for a long time, I know it from experience." . . .

The stock-dove went home and thought the matter over more closely; it occurred to it at once that it must be very gratifying thus to *know* that one's subsistence was assured for a long time, while, on the contrary, it was indeed wretched to live thus constantly in uncertainty, so one never dares to say that one *knows* that one is provided for. . . .

Next morning it awakened earlier than usual, and was now so busy gathering together, that it scarcely got time to eat or to eat its fill. . . . However, no essential change took place with respect to its living. . . . But it had *conceived* a future need; its peace of mind was lost — it had acquired *anxiety for the necessities of life.* From now on the stock-dove became concerned, its feathers lost their sheen, its flight its ease. . . .

At last it devised a cunning plan. One day it flew over and sat on the ridge of the farmer's roof between the tame doves. When it noticed that there was a place where these flew in, it also flew in, for the storeroom must certainly be there. But when the farmer came in the evening and locked the dove-cote, he at once discovered the strange dove. This he then put in a little box by itself until the next day, when it was killed — and freed from anxiety for the necessities of life. . . .

Had the stock-dove been content to be what it was — a bird of the air, then it would have had its living, then would the heavenly Father have fed it, then, in the event of uncertainty, it would have been where it belonged, there where the straight, solitary, sombre trunks are in good understanding with the cooing trill of the stock-dove; then it would have been the one of which the preacher spoke on Sunday, when he repeated the Gospel words: "Behold the fowls of the air, which neither sow nor reap nor gather into barns, yet your heavenly Father feeds them." . . . If the heavenly Father feeds [a person], then he is indeed without anxiety for his subsistence, then he lives not only like the tame doves with the rich peasant, but he lives with that One who is richer than all. He actually dwells with Him, for when heaven and earth are God's house and possession, then man indeed dwells with Him.

It means this: being satisfied with being human, being satisfied with being the humble, the creature, who can just as little support himself as he can create himself. If, on the other hand, man is willing to forget God — and support himself: then we have a care for the necessities of life. It is certainly laudable and pleasing to God that a man sows and harvests and gathers into barns, that he works to find food; but if he is willing to forget God and to believe that he supports himself with his labor, then he becomes uneasy about his livelihood. The richest man who ever lived, if he forgets God, and believes that he supports himself by his labor, has financial anxieties. . . .

To be dependent on his own wealth, that is dependence and heavy bondage; to be dependent on God, absolutely dependent, that is independence. The worried stock-dove foolishly feared to remain absolutely dependent on God, therefore it ceased to be independent and to be the symbol of independence; ceased to be the poor bird of the air, which is absolutely dependent on God. Dependence on God is the only independence, for God has no heaviness; only the earthly and especially the earthly treasure has that.[9]

---

9 *Ibid.*, pp. 188-97.

The Fireworks and the Stars

Human ingenuity has invented a great many things to amuse and divert the mind, and yet the law for this kind of invention mocks the fruitless striving by the self-contradiction of the diversion. The art itself is at the service of impatience; more and more impatiently it learns to compress the multitude of diversions into a short-lived moment: the more this ingenuity increases the more it works against itself, since it appears that as the ingenuity increases, the diversion constantly lasts for a shorter and shorter time.

Let us take an example, where the vain and worldly diversion shows itself as slight and self-contradictory as it is. Fireworks indeed delight the eye and divert the mind when the elaborate, blazing ephemerality is lighted in the darkness of the night. And yet, if it lasts merely one hour the spectator grows weary; if but one brief moment intervenes before each new ignition, then the spectator grows weary. The task of ingenuity is therefore to speed it up faster and faster; the highest, the most perfect performance consists in burning the whole display in a very few minutes. But if the purpose of the diversion is to while away the time, then the contradiction appears clearly. . . .

As those antic flames blaze and immediately vanish into nothing, so must the soul be of him who knows only such diversions: in the moment of diversion he despairs over the length of time it takes.

Ah, how different are the godly diversions! For have you ever seen the star-lit heavens, and have you ever found any more authentic spectacle! . . . As God makes Himself invisible, alas, because of that there are many who perhaps have never really noticed Him: so the starry heaven makes itself, as it were, insignificant; alas, perhaps that is the

reason why there are so many who have never really seen
it. The divine Majesty disdains the visible, false obvious-
ness. . . . Its persuasiveness increases with every moment;
more and more movingly it draws you away from the
temporal; what is to be forgotten sinks into deeper and
deeper oblivion with every moment you continue to ob-
serve the starry heavens.[10]

*The things of the world, like fireworks, are diversions
that share all the shortcomings and futility of diversions.
Simplicity, on the other hand, is like a view of the starry
heavens. Kierkegaard's analogy underlines a point we insisted upon earlier. The starry heavens do not represent
simplicity itself, as though one were to contemplate simplicity and find his reward in doing so. No, the starry
heavens represent God himself, and simplicity is valued
only as a means to that seeing. But neither Kierkegaard
nor the Bible has any opinion about a simplicity that is
treated as an end in itself, detached from and without
reference to the vision of God.*

10*Ibid.*, pp. 201-02.

Chapter Six

IT'S THE LIFE INSIGHTS

This chapter consists of some of Kierkegaard's comments on the simple life, gathered from hither and yon throughout his writings. They have then been excerpted, condensed, pulled into some semblance of order, introduced, and commented upon for presentation here.

From Egghead to Simple Christian

Kierkegaard's reputation as a super-egghead is, as we have suggested, off the mark; but it is not entirely without basis. He could and did write that way — and about the simple life *even. Yet it was not that he was confused, or that he was entranced with high-falutin language; he knew what he was doing (or at least* trying *to do).*

He was working at what he called "indirect communication." His theory was that, in order to communicate with a person, you must first catch him where he is — even if this is not the level on which ultimately you desire to get at him. The trick, then, is to catch his attention through indirect communication and then, with it, lead him to the place where you can address your real concern to him directly. And Kierkegaard knew that there are many people who will not give serious attention to anything unless it is put in very sophisticated terms; so he was willing to talk that way — at least to begin with.

All five of the quotations below are saying pretty much the same thing (and the same thing our first two chapters were saying); but no one would ever guess it simply by comparing their outward forms. The first two are couched in highly rationalized, philosophical terms, with no reference to the Bible and with even the references to God being very much disguised.

But although it runs contrary to the way many moderns value things, Kierkegaard would have insisted that the last three quotations are much the truer *statements of what he has in mind. Real Christian experience, he maintained, does not begin with a simple, biblical, down-to-earth faith that then progresses to the higher and truer level of a more formal and abstract theo-philosophical understanding. Quite the reverse, one grows into Christianity by becoming ever more simple and concrete. The first two quotations are from a work Kierkegaard did not publish under his own name but which he ascribed to a pseudonym who deliberately was portrayed as being less than a Christian. Kierkegaard specified the book as being an example of his "indirect communication."*

Kierkegaard's very career as an author, then, is a powerful witness to his understanding of the simple life — and that in an area we might tend to overlook, namely, simplicity in thought and expression.

Now if for any individual an eternal happiness is his highest good, this will mean that all finite satisfactions are volitionally relegated to the status of what may have to be renounced in favor of an eternal happiness.[11]

---

[11]*Concluding Unscientific Postscript,* trans. by David Swenson and Walter Lowrie (Princeton University Press, 1941), p. 350.

It is important to note that, whenever Kierkegaard speaks of "the eternal" (either here or elsewhere), he customarily means this as a designation of God himself. Likewise, then, "an eternal happiness" refers, not simply to pie in the sky bye and bye, but to the happiness attendant upon one's relationship to God — which, of course, can begin at any time and continue through all times.

In order that the individual may sustain an absolute relationship to the absolute *telos* he must first have exercised himself in the renunciation of relative ends, and only then can there be a question of the ideal task: the simultaneous maintenance of an absolute relationship to the absolute, and a relative relationship to the relative.[12]

When it is said, "Seek ye *first* the kingdom of God," . . . it is required above all that man seek not *first* something else. But what is this "something else" he seeks? It is the temporal. If then he is to seek first God's kingdom, he must freely renounce every temporal goal.[13]

God's kingdom only can be sought when it is sought first; he who does not seek God's kingdom first does not seek it at all.[14]

But if a man seeks the kingdom of God first — *"then shall all these things be added unto him";* they shall be added unto him, for there is only one thing which must be sought: the kingdom of God; neither the thousands of the rich nor the penny of the poor is to be sought — this shall be added unto you.[15]

---

[12]*Ibid.*, p. 386.

[13]*Christian Discourses,* trans. by Walter Lowrie (Oxford University Press, 1940), p. 159.

[14]*Ibid.*, p. 331.

[15]*The Gospel of Suffering*, p. 235.

The Potential for Simplicity

*In this group of quotations, Kierkegaard seems to be
speaking of a fundamental order of simplicity that lies
within human nature even prior to its expression in simple
living or action. Such a judgment is correct but hardly
adequate to Kierkegaard's idea. He makes it plain that,
merely in following natural instinct, man's life does not
express simplicity; the natural drift is all toward shrewd-
ness, cunning, and complexity. It is only through God and
with his help that man can get back to the basic primitiveness for which he was created.*

Every man has a basic primitive disposition (for primitiveness is the possibility of "spirit"). God knows this
best, for it is he who has created it.

All earthly, temporal, worldly cleverness tends to destroy
its own primitiveness.* Christianity aims at following it.

Destroy your own primitiveness, and in all probability
you will get through the world well, perhaps even be a
success — but eternity will denounce you. Follow your
primitiveness, and you will fail in the temporal world;
but eternity will accept you.

*[in the margin]: By primitiveness Christianity of
course does not mean all that trumpery of intellectuality,
being a genius, and the like. No, primitiveness, spirit,
means to stake one's life, first, first, first on the kingdom of
God. The more literally a man can take this in his actions,
the greater is his primitiveness.[16]

There is only one thing which overcomes, which more
than overcomes, from the very beginning has endlessly
overcome, all cunning, that is the simplicity of the gospel,

---

[16]*The Last Years: Journals 1853-55*, trans. by Ronald Gregor Smith
(Harper & Row, 1965), pp. 142-43.

which in its simplicity lets itself be deceived as it were, and yet continues to be the simple. And this too is the edifying feature of the gospel's simplicity, that the Evil could not prevail over it to the point of making it wish to be shrewd. Verily the Evil has won a victory, and a very serious victory, when it has prompted simplicity to wish to be shrewd . . . for the sake of making itself secure. For simplicity is made secure, eternally secure, only by letting itself in its simplicity be deceived, however clearly it sees through the deceit.[17]

Simplicity Is the Choosing of God

When the physician sees that it is all over with the sick man, then one can immediately hear it in his voice; he speaks in passing in a half-whisper, evasively. But, on the contrary, when the physician sees that he can do much, especially that the sick man himself can do much: then he speaks incisively: the severity itself is precisely his admission. . . .

We can speak in many ways about the lilies and the birds; we may speak mildly, movingly, charmingly, affectionately, almost as a poet speaks. . . . But when the Gospel speaks with authority, then it speaks with the earnestness of eternity, then there is no more time to hang about dreaming of the lily, or to look wistfully after the bird. . . .

"No man can serve two masters." And here there can be no doubt about what two the saying refers to. . . . The speech cannot be about his relation to men, about serving a master as his servant, or a wise man as his disciple, but only about serving God or the world. . . . "He must either

---

[17]*Christian Discourses*, p. 372.

hate the one and love the other, or he must hold to the one and despise the other." Consequently love to God is hatred to the world, and love for the world is hatred toward God; consequently this is the tremendous issue — either love or hate. Hence this is the place where the world's most terrible conflict is to be fought. And where is this place? In a man's heart. . . .

Now the sadness is indeed forgotten over the terrible nature of the conflict, but then we reach the glorious thing: *that the man is granted a choice.* . . . A choice. Do you know, my hearer, how in a single word to express anything more glorious; do you know, if you were to talk year out and year in, how to name anything more glorious than a choice, than having a choice! For it is indeed true that the one happiness still consists in choosing rightly, but the choice itself is still the glorious condition. What does the maiden care about a catalogue of all her intended's excellent qualities, if she herself may not choose; and on the other hand, what more glorious thing does she know to say than when she says, whether others praise the beloved's many perfections or mention his many faults: "He is my heart's choice!" . . .

God and the world. Do you know anything greater to set together for a choice! Do you know any more overwhelming and humbling expression of God's indulgence and pardon towards man, than that He sets Himself, in a certain sense, on an equal line of choice with the world, merely in order to allow the man to choose? That God, if language may venture to speak in this way, sets the man free, that He, the eternal Strength, sets free the weak man, for the stronger always frees the weaker. . . .

Man *must* choose; for thus God holds Himself in honor, while He also has a fatherly solicitude for the man. If God has condescended to be that which *may be chosen,* then man *must* also choose — God will not suffer Himself to be mocked. Therefore is it truly so that if a man refrains from choosing, then this is the same thing as presumptuously choosing the world? . . .

No one is to be able to say: "God and mammon, since they are not so unconditionally different, one may in his choice combine both" — for this is to refrain from choosing. . . . No one is able to say: "One can choose a little mammon, and then God too." No, oh, no, that is impudent blasphemy, if anyone were to think that only the one who asks much money, chooses mammon. Ah, the one who asks a farthing without God, a farthing he wishes to have for himself, he chooses mammon. . . .

It is precisely God's presence in the choice which posits the choice: between God and mammon. . . . What is the man to choose? He is to choose the kingdom of God and His righteousness. . . . The right beginning begins with seeking the kingdom of God first; it begins therefore precisely with letting the world be lost. . . . There is no time to gather riches in advance, there is no time to reflect on this question, there is no time to lay up a penny in advance, for the beginning is: to seek first the kingdom of God. . . . He who does not seek it first, does not seek it at all, indifferently, absolutely indifferently, whether he goes to seek a penny or a million.

"God's kingdom and His righteousness." Through the latter the former is described. For God's kingdom is "righteousness, peace and joy in the Holy Spirit." . . . Let then the lily wither, and its beauty become unrecognizable; let the blade of grass fall to earth and the bird fly away; let darkness be upon the fields: God's kingdom does not change with the changing years! Let then the "rest" be needed for a long or short time, let it come abundantly or scantily; let "all these things" have their

moment, when they are dispensed with or possessed, their
moment as the subject for discussion, until they are eternally forgotten in death: God's kingdom is still that which
is to be sought first, but which shall also endure through
all eternities to the last.[18]

*To choose God is all-important; but in the following
we learn that one reason this is so is because God is the
only Master, himself the one true integer, the choice of
whom will serve to integrate the* chooser *as well.*

There is only one master whom a man can serve *wholly*.
For in the choice between two masters it is not true that if
only a man chooses one of the two and then serves him,
no matter which, he is thus serving only one master. . . .
It is not true therefore that one who has chosen to serve
mammon wholly, serves only one master; against his will
he is none the less in the service of the other master, in the
Lord's service. . . . No, a man who has chosen to serve
another master than "the Master," however desperate and
determined his will may be, remains nevertheless in the
service of two masters. And just this self-contradiction is
his punishment, the contradiction of willing the impossible — for it is impossible to serve two masters. . . .

The Christian serves only one Master; and he not merely
serves Him but loves Him, he loves the Lord his God with
all his heart and with all his strength. Just for this reason
he serves Him wholly; for only love unites wholly, unites
the most diverse parties in love, and in this instance unites
man to God who is love. Love is the firmest of all bonds,
for it makes the lover one with the beloved; more firmly
no bond can bind, or so firmly can no bond bind. And the
love which loves God is the bond of perfectness, which in
perfect obedience makes man one with the God he loves.

---

[18]*The Gospel of Suffering*, pp. 225-36.

And the love which loves God is the most beneficial bond, which by keeping a man wholly in God's service saves him from anxieties. This love unifies a man, it makes him eternally in agreement with himself and with the Master who is one; and it unifies a man in likeness to God. . . .

This properly is the hymn of praise, the paean, the song of songs: by joyful and unconditional obedience to praise God when one cannot understand Him. To praise Him upon the day when all goes against thee, when it becomes dark before thine eyes, when others perhaps could easily prove to thee that no God exists — then instead of assuming an air of importance by *proving* that there is a God, humbly to prove that thou dost believe that God exists, to prove it by joyful and unconditional obedience — that is the hymn of praise. The hymn is not something higher than obedience, but obedience is the only true hymn of praise; in obedience the hymn consists, and if the hymn is truth, it is obedience.[19]

The choice is one that integrates *the chooser; but in order for it to do so, Kierkegaard now tells us, that choice must be entirely* voluntary.

Voluntarily to give up all is Christianity. . . . It is actually true that Christianity requires the Christian to give up and forsake all things. This was not required in Old Testament times. . . . But in fact Christianity is also the religion of freedom, it is precisely the voluntary which is the Christian. Voluntarily to give up all is to be convinced of the glory of the good which Christianity promises. . . .

There was a time in Christendom when people thought they could do penance by actually forsaking all things, by

---

19*Christian Discourses*, pp. 85-88.

fleeing to the solitude of the desert, or seeking to be persecuted in the swarming city. There is another way of
doing penance, that of being thoroughly sincere towards
God. . . . I do not know that anywhere it is unconditionally
required of a man in Christendom that to be a Christian
and to become blessed he must in a literal sense forsake
everything, or even sacrifice his life, be executed for the
sake of Christianity. But this I know, that with an insincere
man God can have nothing to do.[20]

*The above point is crucial. It specifies that if one
chooses God out of any motivation other than the sheer
fact that he wants to, that he loves God for His own sake,
that his desire lies totally in the choosing of God . . . unless
this is the motivation, none of the rest follows. Thus, God
cannot be chosen out of a sense of obligation, under the
pressure of fear, according to legalistic prescription, or as
a scheme to win some other benefit. Voluntary, sincere
desire marks the only true choice.*

*The quotation to follow goes on to point out that this
choice necessarily manifests itself as absolute* obedience —
as absolutely voluntary *obedience, it goes without saying.*

If God were to speak or could speak of Himself as if He
were not absolutely No. 1, as if He were not the only one,
absolutely everything, but merely another something or
another, one who indulged the hope that he also might
perhaps be taken into account along with other things —
in such case God would have lost Himself, lost the notion
of what He is, and He would not be God. . . .

There is one thing the lilies and the birds absolutely do
not understand, namely, half-measures — which, alas, most

---

[20]*Ibid.,* pp. 186-95.

men understand best. That a little disobedience, that this
might not be absolute disobedience, is something the lilies
and the birds cannot and will not understand. That the
least, the very least disobedience, might in truth have any
other name than . . . contempt of God — that the lilies
and the birds cannot and will not understand. . . .

Though the place allotted the lily is as disadvantageous
as possible, so that it easily can be foreseen that it will be
entirely superfluous all its life long, not be noticed by any
one who might rejoice in it; though the place and the
environment is (why, here I have forgotten that it is the
lily I am talking about!) — is so "desperately" disadvantageous that not only is it not sought out but is avoided,
nevertheless the obedient lily puts up obediently with its
circumstances and shoots up in all its beauty. We men, or
a man in the situation of the lily, would surely say, "It is
hard, it is not to be endured, when one is a lily and beautiful as a lily, then to be allotted a place in such a situation,
to bloom there in an environment which is as unfavorable
as possible." . . .

But the lily thinks differently, it thinks thus: "I myself
have not been able to determine the situation and the
circumstances, and so it is not in the remotest way my
affair; that I stand where I stand is God's will." . . . For
the lily is, in spite of the environment, itself, because it
is absolutely obedient to God; and because it is absolutely
obedient to God, therefore it is absolutely care-free, as
only the absolutely obedient (especially under such conditions) can be. And because it is fully and completely
itself, and absolutely care-free (two things which cor-
respond to one another directly and inversely), therefore
it is beautiful. Only by absolute obedience can one with
absolute accuracy hit upon the "spot" where one is to
stand, and when one hits upon it absolutely one under-

stands that it is absolutely indifferent whether the spot be a dunghill. . . .

If thou art absolutely obedient to God, then there is no ambiguity in thee, and if there is no ambiguity in thee, then art thou mere simplicity before God. But one thing there is which all Satan's cunning and all the snares of temptation cannot take by surprise, and that is simplicity. What Satan spies with keenness of sight as his prey (but what never is found in the lilies and the birds), what all temptation aims at, certain of its prey (but what never is found in the lilies and the birds) — is the ambiguous. Where the ambiguous is, there is temptation, and there it proves only too easily the stronger. But where the ambiguous is, there also, in one way or another, is disobedience down at the bottom. . . . But the man who with absolute obedience hides himself in God is absolutely safe; from his hiding-place he can see the devil, but the devil cannot see him.[21]

That obedience, as an escape from ambiguity, is itself the source of man's true freedom . . . this is indeed a thought to ponder. Yet, still on the theme of obedience, Kierkegaard tells us now that the first movement indicated is not to get out and do thus and so but to become quiet so that God can speak his will and be heard.

"Seek ye first God's kingdom and his righteousness."

What does this mean, what have I to do, or what sort of effort is it that can be said to seek or pursue the kingdom of God? Shall I try to get a job suitable to my talents and powers in order thereby to exert an influence? No, thou shalt *first* seek God's kingdom. Shall I then give all my fortune to the poor? No, thou shalt *first* seek God's king-

---

[21]*Ibid.,* pp. 335-44.

dom. Shall I then go out to proclaim this teaching to the
world? No, thou shalt *first* seek God's kingdom. But then
in a certain sense it is nothing I shall do. Yes, certainly,
in a certain sense it is nothing; thou shalt in the deepest
sense make thyself nothing, become nothing before God,
learn to keep silent; in this silence is the beginning, which
is, *first* to seek God's kingdom. . . .

It is man's superiority over the beast to be able to speak;
but in relation to God it can easily become the ruin of
man who is able to speak that he is too willing to speak. . . .
This the true man of prayer knows well, and he who was
not the true man of prayer learned perhaps precisely this
by praying. . . . In proportion as he became more and more
earnest in prayer, he had less and less to say, and in the
end he became quite silent. He became silent — indeed,
what is if possible still more expressly the opposite of
speaking, he became a hearer. He had supposed that to
pray is to speak; he learnt that to pray is not merely to be
silent but to hear. And so it is; to pray is not to hear oneself speak, but it is to be silent, and to remain silent, to
wait, until the man who prays hears God. . . . Not as though
prayer always began with silence (which we have seen is
not the case) , but when prayer has really become prayer
it has become silence. Seek first God's kingdom — that
means, Pray! . . .

That thou in silence mightest forget thyself, what thy
name is, thine own name, the renowned name, the pitiful
name, the insignificant name, for the sake of praying in
silence to God, "Hallowed be *Thy* name!" That thou in
silence mightest forget thyself, thy plans, the great, the
all-comprehensive plans, or the petty plans regarding thy
life and its future, for the sake of praying in silence to
God, "*Thy* kingdom come!" That thou in silence mightest
forget thy will, thy self-will, for the sake of praying in

silence to God, "*Thy* will be done!" Yea, if thou couldst
learn from the lilies and the birds to become perfectly
silent before God, what might not the Gospel help thee to
accomplish, then nothing would be impossible for thee![22]

*And thus to choose so completely that all other concerns
and interests are forsaken and fall into silence ... this is the
highest praise man can give to God.*

In case there was a lover who with the most beautiful
and glowing expressions extolled his lady's perfection and
superiority, and there was another lover who said not a
single word about this, but only, "Behold, for her sake I
have forsaken all" — which of these two spoke most gloriously in her praise? For nothing runs so fast as the tongue,
and nothing is easier than to let the tongue run, and only
this is equally easy: by the help of the tongue to run away
from oneself, in what one says to be many, many thousand
miles ahead of oneself. If therefore thou wouldst extol
Christianity — oh, do not wish for thyself the tongues of
angels, nor the art of all the poets, nor the eloquence of
all orators: in the same degree that thy life shows how
much thou hast forsaken for the sake of it, in that same
degree dost thou extol Christianity.[23]

The Difficulty of Doing It Right

*In one sense the simple life is so easy — just choosing
God and letting other things fall into place. But in another
sense it is so difficult, because it actually involves a denying
of one's self and a following of Christ. Yet, easy or difficult,
the outcome is the greatest.*

22*Ibid.*, pp. 322-30.
23*Ibid.*, p. 185.

To bear one's cross means to deny one's self. . . . To deny one's self is a *slow* and *burdensome* task. . . . One good deed, one high-minded resolution, does not constitute self-denial. . . . Christ did not say to the rich young man: "If you wish to be perfect, then sell all your goods and give the money to the poor." . . . He says: "Go away and sell what you have and give it to the poor, and come, take up the cross and follow me" (Mark 10:21). Hence, the fact of selling one's goods and giving the money to the poor is not taking up the cross, or it is at most the beginning, the good beginning. . . . It is, since the language permits an innocent ingenuousness: *taking up the cross.* The next step, the long-continued process is: *to bear one's cross.* It must be done daily, not once for all; and there must be nothing, nothing that the disciple is not willing to give up in self-denial.

Perhaps there was someone willing to do what the rich young man did not do, in the hope of thereby perfecting the highest, and yet who did not become a disciple because he stood still, "turned and looked back" — at his great achievement; or, if he did go forward, still did not become a disciple, because he thought he had done something so great that trivialities did not matter. . . .

To follow Christ, then, means denying one's self, and hence it means *walking the same way* as Christ walked in the humble form of a servant — needy, forsaken, mocked, not loving worldliness and not loved by the worldly minded. . . . In the crucial pressure of life, it seems a difficult, an impossible thing to live in such a way; impossible even to decide whether anyone actually does live this way. But let us not forget that it is eternity which is to judge how the task was performed. . . .

The proof that the eternal happiness exists is quite gloriously set forth by Paul; for there can be absolutely

no doubt that without it he would have been the most
wretched of men! If, on the other hand, a man seeks to
assure himself in this world, seeks to secure himself the
advantage of this world, then is his assurance that there
is an eternal happiness hereafter not quite convincing;
it scarcely convinces others, it has scarcely convinced
himself.[24]

Simplicity for the Poor

*The sheer fact that one is poor is not in itself any indica-
tion that he is living in Christian simplicity and thus
knows the truth of Jesus' "Be not anxious!" Indeed,
poverty can carry a particular anxiety of its own.*

What is the anxiety of poverty if it is not that of desiring
to be rich? . . . To be without anxiety, yea, that is a difficult
gait to go, almost like walking upon the water; but if
thou art able to believe, it can nevertheless be done. . . .
So it is the Christian goes *his* gait; he turns his eyes upward, he looks away from danger, in poverty he is without
the anxiety of poverty. But he who desires to be rich — his
thought is constantly upon the ground, with his anxiety
about earthly things; he walks with bowed head, looking
constantly before him, if perchance he might find riches.[25]

*Yet true Christian simplicity can free the poor man
from his anxiety and even make him rich.*

What shall we eat? or, What shall we drink? — After all
these things do the heathen seek; for *the Christian does*

24*The Gospel of Suffering*, pp. 10-20.
25*Christian Discourses*, p. 24.

not have this anxiety. . . . We are talking about the Christian who is poor, about the poor Christian. He is poor, but he has not this anxiety, so is poor and yet not poor. . . . What then does the poor Christian live on? On the *daily bread.* . . . But therefore he has also, however poor he may be, something more to live on than the daily bread, which to him has an added flavor, a value, a satisfying quality; . . . for the Christian indeed prays for it, and so he knows that the daily bread is *from God.* . . .

He says, "For me it is enough, it is from Him, that is, from God." . . . He believes that he has a Father in heaven who every day openeth His bountiful hand and fillest all things living (him included) with blessing; yet what he seeks is not the satisfaction of his appetite, it is the heavenly Father. . . . He constantly bears in mind that a life of holiness was led here on earth in poverty, that "He" was hungry in the desert and thirsted on the cross; so that not only can one live in poverty, but in poverty one can *live.* — Hence he prays, it is true, for the daily bread, and gives thanks for it, but to pray and give thanks is to him more important than food, and is indeed his meat, as it was Christ's "meat to do the Father's will." . . .

To be able to pray and to give thanks is precisely to be existent for God. . . . And [the poor Christian's] riches indeed increase with every time he prays and gives thanks, with every time it becomes clearer that he exists for God and God for him; whereas earthly riches become poorer and poorer with every time the rich man forgets to pray and to give thanks. . . .

But then indeed the poor Christian is rich? Yes, certainly he is rich, and thou shalt recognize him by the fact that he does not wish to talk about his earthly poverty, but rather of his heavenly riches. . . . The Christian shares as it were with God; he lets God take thought for meat and drink and all such things, while he seeks God's kingdom and His righteousness.[26]

Simplicity for the Rich

Kierkegaard here essays to tread the very tricky territory we tried to nagivate earlier. The simple life dare not be defined simply as an arbitrary ceiling regarding how much a man may own and still be a Christian. Yet neither dare it become the license for a person to gather everything his heart desires and claim God's approval in doing it.

One thing is quite arbitrary and that is to make poverty into piety, as though it were something in itself. . . . It is quite a different matter when poverty is related to an idea, in the service of which man places his life.[27]

It is not given to everyone, nor is everyone asked unconditionally to live, in the strictest sense of the word, in poverty and abasement. But he must be honest, he must openly admit that that is above him, and so take a childlike joy in the gentler conditions, since ultimately grace is the same for all. But the situation must not be twisted around, people must not be conceited and say: it is more perfect to include worldliness.[28]

Kierkegaard makes a good point here: If a Christian finds it necessary and permissible to retain a degree of worldly wealth, let him at least be honest enough to recognize that he is indulging the faith. But it is sheer hypocrisy

26*Ibid.*, pp. 18-21.

27*The Journals of Kierkegaard*, trans. by Alexander Dru (Oxford University Press, 1938), entry #1124.

28*Ibid.*, entry #1113.

*when many Christians keep their wealth and then make
out as if it were a reward for their faithfulness and a mark
of God's blessing.*

*Yet, in our next selection, he goes on to argue that, al-
though the gospel may not* require *a literal making of
oneself poor as the only way to Christian simplicity, it
nevertheless is the case that literal poverty represents the
surest and safest way there.*

Christianity has never taught that to be literally a lowly
man is synonymous with being a Christian, nor that from
the literal condition of lowliness there is direct transition
as a matter of course to becoming a Christian; neither has
it taught that if the man of worldly position were to give
up all his power, he therefore would be a Christian. But
from literal lowliness to the point of becoming a Christian
there is however only one step. The position of being
literally a lowly man is by no means an unfavorable
preparation for becoming a Christian; the position of
being in possession of the advantages of outward circumstance is a circuitous path, which for the more scrupulous
makes necessary a double preparation. . . .

One who has the advantages of outward circumstance
helps himself by becoming literally poor, despised and
lowly. If he does not do this he must with all the more inward concern watch over himself. . . . Christianity has
never required unconditionally of anyone that he should
literally give up the advantages of outward circumstance,
it has proposed to men rather a little precautionary rule.[29]

*We shall discover that the "precautionary rule" Kierke-
gaard has in mind is the attitude of "as if not." However,
he will insist that true Christian simplicity is a possibility
even for the well-to-do.*

---

[29]*Christian Discourses,* pp. 57-58.

But is abundance then an anxiety? . . . For riches and abundance come hypocritically clad in sheep's clothing, pretending to be security against anxieties, and they become then the object of anxiety, of "the anxiety"; they secure a man against anxieties just about as well as the wolf which is put to tending the sheep secures them . . . against the wolf. . . .

[The bird of the air] teaches us the surest way to avoid the anxiety of riches and abundance, namely, not to lay up riches and abundance — bearing in mind that one is a traveler; and in the second place, it teaches us (what is especially appropriate to this discourse) , in abundance to be ignorant of the fact that one has abundance — bearing in mind that one is a traveler. . . .

In connection with abundance, thought can take from the rich man the thought of *possession,* the thought that he owns and possesses this wealth and abundance as *his.* . . . When I do not know what I am to live on tomorrow, I evidently possess nothing. But when I reflect that I might die tonight, "this very night," then I possess nothing, however rich I may be. To be rich I must possess something until the morrow, etc., must be secured *for* the morrow; but to be rich I must also be assured *of* the morrow. Take away riches, and then no longer can I be called rich; but take away the morrow, and then too, alas, I no longer can be called rich. . . .

So far from calling the earthly riches "mine," the rich Christian realizes that they are God's, and that they are to be administered as far as possible in accordance with the proprietor's wish, administered with the proprietor's indifference to money and money value, administered by giving them away at the right time and place. . . .

He has no anxiety in gathering abundance, for he does not care to gather abundance; he has no anxiety in retaining, for it is easy enough to retain what one has not, and he is as one who has not; he has no anxiety about losing, for he indeed is as one who has not; he has no anxiety for the fact that others possess more, for he is as one who possesses nothing; and he has no anxiety about what he shall leave to his heirs. . . . As ignorant as the poor Christian is of his earthly poverty, just so ignorant is the rich Christian of his earthly riches; as the former does not talk of his earthly poverty, so he too does not talk of earthly riches; they both talk of one and the same thing, of the heavenly riches. . . . [The rich Christian] keeps constantly in mind that He who possessed all the riches of the world gave up all that He possessed and lived in poverty, and so again in ignorance of all the riches that are possessed. . . .

The bird is — well, if it is rich, it is ignorant that it is rich; the rich Christian *became* ignorant of it, he is rich, poor, rich; the rich heathen is poor, poor, poor. . . . When one is rich there is one way of becoming rich: that of becoming ignorant of one's riches, of becoming poor. The bird's way is the shortest, that of the Christian the most blessed. According to the teaching of Christianity, there is only one rich man, namely, the Christian; every one else is poor, both the poor man and the rich. A man is most healthy when he does not notice at all or know that he has a body, and the rich man is in health when, as healthy as the bird, he knows nothing of his earthly riches; but when he knows of it, when it is the only thing he knows, then he is lost. When the rich Christian became entirely ignorant of his earthly riches he gained more than the bird, he gained heaven; when the rich heathen became entirely and solely conscious of his riches he lost what no bird loses when it falls to the ground, he lost heaven.[30]

---

[30]*Ibid.*, pp. 27-39.

On the Throwing Off of Anxiety

Simplicity is the cure for anxiety. One way it does this is by getting rid of "tomorrow."

From whatever height the bird surveyed the whole world, and whatever it saw, it never saw "the next day." . . . There is no yesterday and no tomorrow for the bird, it lives but one day, and the lily blooms but one day. Consequently the bird has no anxiety for the next day. But anxiety for the next day is precisely what self-torment is, and hence the bird is without the anxiety of self-torment. For what is self-torment? It is the worry which today (having enough worry of its own) does not have. . . .

The Gospel says that "every day has enough worries of its own." . . . It assumes that with the daily worries a man can manage to get along. It says therefore, in effect, every day *shall* have its worries. . . . Every day shall have its worry, that is to say, take care to be free from the next day's worry, accept tranquilly and gratefully the worry of today, thou dost get off easily with that . . . by becoming free from the next day's worry. . . .

One who rows a boat turns his back to the goal toward which he labours. So it is with the next day. When by the help of eternity a man lives absorbed in today, he turns his back to the next day. The more he is eternally absorbed in today, the more decisively does he turn his back upon the next day, so that he does not see it at all. If he turns around, eternity is confused before his eyes, it becomes the next day. But if for the sake of labouring more effectually towards the goal (eternity) he turns his back, he does not see the next day at all, whereas by the help of eternity he sees quite clearly today and its task. . . .

Hence when the Christian works, or when he prays, he

talks only of today: he prays for daily bread "today," for a
blessing upon his work "today," that he may avoid the
snares of the evil one "today," that he may come nearer to
God's kingdom "today." . . . To live thus, to cram today
with eternity and not with the next day, the Christian has
learnt and continues to learn (for the Christian is always
learning) from the Pattern. . . . He had Eternity with Him
in the day that is called today, hence the next day had no
power over Him, it had no existence for Him. It had no
power over Him before it came, and when it came and
was the day that is called today it had no other power over
Him than that which was the Father's will, to which He
consented with eternal freedom, and to which He obediently bowed.[31]

*What follows represents a significant insight regarding
anxiety. That man can be anxious (and yet also find the
means of rising above his anxiety) marks a real superiority
over the birds and lilies who are free of anxiety only because they do not have the capacity for such.*

It is a perfection *to be able* to have a care for the necessities of life — in order to overcome this fear, in order to
let faith and confidence drive out fear, so that one is in
truth without a care for the necessities of life in the un-
concern of faith. For only this freedom from care on the
part of faith is in the divine sense the soaring, whose beautiful but imperfect symbol is the easy flight of the bird. . . .
   The bird that is without subsistence cares, is then the
symbol of the human, and yet the human, through being
able to have these cares, is far more perfect than the symbol. Therefore the human never dares forget that the One
who referred him to the bird of the air, as to a primary, a

---

[31]*Ibid.*, pp. 73-79.

childish instruction, that precisely He in earnestness and truth is the real symbol, the true, essential human symbol of perfection. . . . For when it is said, "The birds of the air have nests and foxes have holes, but the Son of man has not where to lay his head," then there is mentioned a condition which is far more helpless than that of a bird, and is also itself conscious of this. But then, with the consciousness of this, to be without a nest, without a place in which to seek refuge, then—to be without anxiety: aye, this is the exalted image of creation, this is man's divine pattern. . . .

"*The bird sows not, it reaps not, nor does it gather into barns*"; that is to say, the bird does not *labor*. But is this then a perfection, not to work at all? . . . To work is the perfection of the human. Through working the human being resembles God, who also works. And if, then, a man works for food, we shall not foolishly say that he supports himself; we shall rather say, simply in order to recall how glorious it is to be human: "He works with God for food. He works with God, hence he is God's fellow-worker." The bird is not that; it gets its food, but it is not God's fellow-laborer.[32]

Kierkegaard has just made it plain that the simple life, far from implying a freedom from work, incorporates work as a privilege through which the Christian helps God in the dispelling of anxiety. He pursues the thought further in the beautiful little illustration that follows.

"Consider the lilies of the field; they sew not, neither do they spin" — and yet the most skilful seamstress who sews for herself, or a princess who with the use of the costliest fabric has her sewing done by the most skilful seamstress,

---

[32]*The Gospel of Suffering*, pp. 213-19.

or Solomon in all his glory, was not arrayed like one of
these. So then there is one who sews and spins for the
lilies? That indeed there is: God in heaven. But as for man,
he sews and spins. "Yes, necessity is enough to teach him
that, necessity teaches naked women to spin." Fie upon
thee, that thou canst think so meanly of thy labour, of
what it is to be a man, so meanly of God and of existence
— as if it were nothing but a house of correction!

No, consider the lilies of the field, learn from them,
learn to understand what thou knowest: thou knowest that
it is man who spins and sews, learn from the lilies to understand that nevertheless really, even when it is man who
spins and sews, it is God who spins and sews. Dost thou
think that the seamstress, if she understands this, will
become less diligent at her work and in it, that she will lay
her hands in her lap and think: "If after all it is really God
who spins and sews, the best thing for me is to be free, to
be liberated from this unreal spinning and sewing"? If so,
then this seamstress is a foolish little maiden, not to say
a saucy wench, in whom God can take no pleasure, and
who can take no pleasure in the lilies, and well deserves
to have the good Lord show the door, and then she would
see what will become of her. But this seamstress, our own
dear lovable seamstress with her childlike piety, understands that only when she herself sews, is it God who
will sew for her, and hence she becomes all the more
diligent at her work, for the fact that by constantly sewing
she constantly must understand — oh, blissful pleasantry!
— that it is God who sews every stitch, for the fact that by
sewing constantly she must constantly understand — oh,
the seriousness of it! — that it is God who sews every
stitch.[33]

---

[33]For Self-Examination, trans. by Walter Lowrie (Princeton University
Press, 1944), p. 192.

Yet, in the final analysis, sheer freedom from anxiety is not what Christian simplicity is all about. No, what it is all about is joy in the Lord.

He whose joy is dependent upon certain conditions is not joy itself, his joy is in fact dependent upon conditions and is conditioned by them. But he who is joy itself is unconditionally joyful, just as, to state the converse proposition, he who is unconditionally joyful is joy itself. . . . For by the help of conditions, even if it were of all conditions, it is impossible indeed to be more than or otherwise than conditionally joyful. . . .

There is a saying of the Apostle Peter which the lilies and the birds have laid to heart, and, simple as they are, they take it quite literally, just this it is that helps them. There is an immense force in this saying when it is taken quite literally; when it is not taken literally, exactly according to the letter, it is more or less powerless, and at last only an unmeaning phrase; but it absolutely requires simplicity to take it absolutely with perfect literalness. "Cast *all* your care UPON GOD." . . .

And indeed this is quite natural, for God the Almighty supports the whole world and all the world's care (including that of the lilies and the birds) with infinite ease. What indescribable joy! — joy over God the Almighty. . . . For this is the absolute joy, to adore the almighty power with which God the Almighty bears all thy care and sorrow as easily as nothing. And this also is the absolute joy, the next one, which in fact the Apostle subjoins, adoringly to dare to believe that "God careth for thee." The absolute joy is precisely joy over God, over whom and in whom thou canst always rejoice. If in this relationship thou art not absolutely joyful, the fault lies absolutely in thee, in thy lack of dexterity in casting thy care upon Him, in thine unwillingness to do it, in thy self-conceit, in short, it lies in the fact that thou art not like the lilies and the birds. . . .

And if thou couldst learn to be entirely like the lilies and the birds — ah, and if I could learn it — then would also the prayer of truth be true in thee and in me, the last prayer in "the Prayer" which (a model of all true prayer, which indeed prays itself joyful, and more joyful, and absolutely joyful) at last has nothing, nothing whatever more to pray for or to desire, but with absolute joyfulness concludes with prayer and worship, the prayer: "For thine is the kingdom and the power and the glory." Yes, *His* is the kingdom; and therefore thou art to be absolutely silent, lest thou mightest make it disturbingly noticeable that thou dost exist, but that with absolute silence thou mayest express the fact that the kingdom is His. And *His* is the power; and therefore thou art to be absolutely obedient and art with absolute obedience to bear with everything, for His is the power. And *His* is the glory; therefore in all that thou doest and in all that thou endurest, thou hast absolutely one thing more to do; to give Him the glory, for the glory is His.[34]

---

[34]*Christian Discourses*, pp. 348-55.

PART III

According to Yours Truly

Chapter Seven

WHY DIDN'T YOU DO WHAT
WE WANTED YOU TO?

Sure, I know what you wanted me to do; I've known all along. You wanted me to give a bunch of specific, concrete suggestions on how to go about living simply, draw you a picture of what a simple life might look like, give you something you can get your hands on and your teeth into.

Well, I'm not going to do it — and, note well, neither Jesus nor Kierkegaard did it either.

I'll tell you why not! First (but definitely not foremost) , to go into specific detail is a sure way to date the book and make its message a very transitory thing. Conversely, it is amazing how relevant and timely are Jesus' teachings two thousand years later and Kierkegaard's interpretations more than a century after they were written.

Second (and much more foremostly) , our major thesis has been that Christian simplicity is not *primarily* a matter of the outward arrangements of life style. Seeking *first* the kingdom cuts in at a different level. But now, whatever we might do in the way of making concrete suggestions could have the effect of undermining the point we truly are concerned to make. Now, by implication, there would be *two* ways of living the simple life: either by seeking first the kingdom *or* by following the author's counsels on what that life looks like.

But be very clear, this is not to say that it is immaterial whether the simple life has a concrete manifestation or not. No, no, no! It is incredible that a person could freely and wholeheartedly choose God and become absolutely obedient to him without it making some change in his relationship to things of the world. If some sort of outward change did not take place, it rightly could be suspected whether he had actually chosen God. That change, of course, will be in the direction of simplicity, a lessened evaluation of what the world promotes as important. Yet, nevertheless, no one can dictate specifics to another; each person, with God's help, will have to evolve *his* style of simple living for himself. And at this point there is no reason at all why a theologian and Bible teacher should be looked to as a source of wisdom or expertise.

Third, whatever we might do here in the way of describing a particular style of simplicity inevitably would give the impression that this is *the* way to do it. But the truth is that there are almost numberless ways of doing it.

I could, for example, exuberate about one demonstration with which I am well familiar. The Society of Brothers (*Bruderhof*) is a Christian community in which the members have renounced private ownership, pooled their resources, and moved the focus of their lives entirely away from concern over "things." I have never seen a more authentic and attractive witness to Christian simplicity. Thank God for these people; and God bless anyone who chooses to go this direction. *But* I am not going to be put into the position of implying that any Christian who does not choose to go this route is somehow falling short of Jesus' teaching and the Christian demand regarding simplicity.

I could describe some old-age pensioners I know — people who live on a very meager income and who never have been very far above that level but who, in their love for God, are as free and content and even *rich* as any other person you could name.

I could talk about some college kids whose poverty (I hope and believe) is not simply temporary and of the necessity of the moment. They are (I hope and believe) committed to the Lord and through him to a continuance of this style of life.

I could talk about the home in which I grew up. The most consistent and dependable occasion for argument at our house came at check-writing time each month. Pop would opine that he thought we could afford to give the church a little extra this time, something beyond our normal pledge and tithe. Mom would respond that we had better hang onto that money until we were sure we didn't need it. And considering the total budget involved, I am sure that any dispassionate observer would have said that, if our "needing it" was the criterion, the church should not have expected any at all.

(By the way, if, as counselors seem now to be saying, money problems are as much as an inevitable point of contention between husband and wife, I would recommend to any couple that they go for this argument that my parents have hassled for years and undoubtedly still are hassling, even though I am not around to hear it any more and so have had to institute the same hassle in my own home.)

I could talk about what I picked up out of that home background. I could describe how uncomfortable I get and how out of place I feel even walking through a plush hotel, let alone staying in one. I could tell how a good meal is ruined for me if I have to pay more than two dollars (or at most two-and-a-half) for it; my stomach is saying, "Enjoy, enjoy!" but my conscience, more loudly, is saying, "Shame on you, waster!"

But, you know, right here lies precisely the trouble with this whole line of thought. I frankly don't know how much my attitude and reactions are motivated by a love of God and how much merely by the psychological conditioning of a fortunate upbringing. I suspect that it is strongly the latter. And it is a sad, sad day when a guy gets a halo just for being *cheap!*

So we dare not measure Christian simplicity by merely external standards; and we dare not lift up certain modes of simplicity in a way that would seem to belittle those whose circumstances and experience have led them into quite different modes of what might well be an equally Christian life.

Finally, there is no lack of information today regarding the outward details of simple living. Christianity can and must provide the *inner motivation* of the simple life; but when we turn to talk about *outward details,* Christianity is of no use at all and shouldn't even be expected to offer help. Now we have moved into the sphere that rightly and appropriately belongs to secular science and technique.

Just try to think, not of how many different books, periodicals, pamphlets, lectures, classes, films, and programs but how many different *kinds* of these are available and relevant to the building of a simple life style. One can start (if this is his "thing") with the *Whole Earth Catalog* and the *Dome Books* and move out from that point. There is, then, all of the ecology literature. Then there is Ralph Nader and no end of consumer guides. There are discount plans, buying clubs, books listing things one can get for free, and schemes for beating the market on all fronts. There is literature on nutrition, health foods, how to cut your grocery bills, etc., etc. There are how-to-do-it books and articles for building or sewing rather than buying almost anything you might care to name. There is stuff on family style and the psychological simplifying of interpersonal relations. There is material regarding family planning and population control. There are health and exercise books and those instructing in the simple human pleasures of massage, sex, etc. There are everywhere articles and books about persons and families who have cut out from the social mass in search of a more simple and individual style of living. There is . . . well, I don't know what all there is; undoubtedly I have missed some major categories; and the best word to describe the whole is "etcetera." Truly, one of the most unsimple things about our current society is the great glut of stuff we have turned out in the promotion of simplicity.

Now if anyone thinks it necessary and wise for the author of this modest book to try to sort out that can of worms he has another guess coming. It will have to be a case of every man for himself; and theological principles will be of very little help. The decisions will need to be made in terms of practicality, empirical testing, trial and error, and even individual taste.

Within this mass of information, there certainly is that which can be of help to the Christian as he strives to simplify his life; but that statement is not to be taken as a blanket recommendation of all this literature — and not even as a recommendation of any particular item within it. This material also carries some inherent dangers for the seeker of Christian simplicity.

For one thing, consider that none of it is presented

under the motivation of setting one's mind on the kingdom of God before everything else. No, the assumed
motive behind it all is what we earlier called "hedonism,"
the search for the sensual (and monetary) satisfactions
that simplicity itself can bring. So be careful; the secular
emphasis can trap a person into seeking first the simple
life, thus making it into an idol that displaces God rather
than opening the way to him. For instance, it seems
apparent that many people relate more truly to Adelle
Davis than to Jesus Christ as Saviour — if the granting of
unquestioning obedience for one's salvation is the test.
The achievement of Christian simplicity is not measured
by how well a person masters any aspect of this literature
and practices it.

Also, because the simplicity thing has taken on the
proportions of a fad, much of what it has produced is
just plain inaccurate and misleading. It would not be
wise, for example, to buy every counsel that has been
uttered in the name of "ecology." The whole matter of
organic food calls for a second look. In many respects it
does not measure up as a move toward simplicity: it is
more expensive than customary foods; if society as a
whole were to move this way, it would cut agriculture
production to the place that more rather than fewer people
in our world would have to starve; it has not been scientifically proven that it is all that much more nutritious.
Watch out, too, for do-it-yourself projects; how many men
have spent much more for shop equipment than the
worth of anything they ever produced with it? And again,
there are many situations in which it is not true that home
gardening represents any kind of saving. Finally, the
ethics of some corner-cutting and discount plans must be
closely examined.

In short, the Christian's finding of simplicity is going

to call not only for spiritual acumen and commitment but also for practical care and wisdom — rather than being just an enthusiastic plunge into today's simplicity cult.

We said earlier that every person will have to find his own way to what Christian simplicity is to be for him. That still holds, but there is a modification that should be considered. There was no intention of suggesting that it is impossible for us to be of help to one another in this area. The final style design will have to be one's own, but brotherly counsel and discussion can be most helpful in getting one to that point. This is something the church could provide: the opportunity for seeking Christians to get together in intimate fellowship for the purpose of sharing with, challenging, and even disciplining one another in a mutual search for the life style that can best express the relationship to God that takes priority over all else.

And the effort need not stop with merely talking together, either. Such a group might be able to find cooperative services and possibly even cooperative ownerships that would have the effect of simplifying the lives of all.

This book has explored only the theological and spiritual dynamics of Christian simplicity. But the possibilities regarding practical details are wide open — and are much more than any one book ever could handle. They are there for the taking. Nevertheless, we Christians need to keep very aware of our inveterate tendency to assume that our theological understanding and spiritual condition already are what they ought to be and that all we need now are a few instructions on what to *do*. Yet, as regards the gospel ideal of simplicity, this activist concern definitely is the minor and secondary consideration; and we would do well to place our major emphasis where the gospel places its. Therefore, set your mind upon God's

kingdom before everything else, and all the rest — including guidance as to what your simplicity should look like
— will come to you as well.

Chapter Eight

IT REALLY IS THE LIFE!

All the way through this book we have been careful to distinguish between *Christian* simplicity and the current *secular* flirtation with simplicity — and that on the grounds that the Christian mode is motivated by something quite other than "hedonism." We have not denied the conviction that many people would indeed find a simple style of life to be sensuously and psychologically satisfying; we *have* denied that there is anything particularly *Christian* about such a motivation.

This we have said (and over and over and over again, it must be confessed). And yet, at this late stage of the game, we are going to propose that *the sole motive of Christian simplicity is* HEDONISM (if that it can be called) ; and in doing so we will not be reneging at all on what we so carefully insisted earlier.

The trumpet note, which at this point we intend for our crescendo and finale, was at least implied in our biblical texts, although we didn't make a great deal of it at the time. It was, however, Kierkegaard who made it explicit and emphatic. The motive of Christian simplicity is not the enjoyment of simplicity itself; that and any other earthly benefit that comes along are part of the "all the rest." But the sole motive of Christian simplicity is the enjoyment of God himself (and if that be *hedonism,* let's make the most of it!) — it is "the view of the stars," "the contemplation of the heavens rather than of fireworks"; it is "the absolute joy" — which is precisely "joy over God, over whom and in whom thou canst always rejoice."

More specifically, Christian simplicity is so to use "things" that, first, they do not interfere with one's absolute joy *in God,* and, second, they actually point toward and contribute to *that* joy. When "things" are given their proper evaluation as being creations of and gifts from the God who loves us and supplies us with every good, then they can operate as integral contributions to that joy. Our task is to receive them in such a way that, as with the reception of any gift, our appreciation focuses on the *giver* rather than on our possession of the gift itself.

So Christian simplicity is not an anxious scrupulosity about possessions (either anxiety about getting and holding them *or about keeping them below a certain "Christian level*) : rather, it is a joyous *freedom* regarding them. When life becomes focused upon God instead of "things," one not only is *freed from* all the anxieties that attend possession, but he also is *made free to* use "things" with all the blessing and joy for which they were created and given to us in the first place.

But in the final analysis this joy must root in God himself and in the prayer of absolute joy "which at last has nothing, nothing whatever more to pray for or to desire, but concludes with absolute joyfulness in the prayer: 'For thine is the kingdom and the power and the glory.' . . . And *His* is the glory; therefore in all that thou doest and in all that thou endurest, thou hast absolutely one thing more to do; to give Him the glory, for the glory is His."

So give it a try, brothers, for, simply put, it's the life!

A

0